The 500 Hidden Secrets of
BUDAPEST

INTRODUCTION

This book lists the places in Budapest the author would recommend to friends if they asked him where to go in his native city. *The 500 Hidden Secrets of Budapest* will help you discover, for example, the 5 next-generation 'ruin bars', 5 intriguing memorial plaques, and 5 great contemporary statues. The aim is to reveal the secret gems that a lot of people don't know about but that are at the same time very characteristic of Budapest, like the visible remains of the medieval city walls, the building that's an exact copy of a palace in Florence, or the intriguing statue in a metro station.

This guide will help you discover the city's past but also the many different aspects of its present. Did you know for example that Budapest is the only large city in the world that is a spa city? That it has a beautiful zoo with a dozen authentic art nouveau animal houses, and half a dozen symphonic orchestras? And that it just experienced something of a revolution in the food and drinks scene, with the opening of several trendy gastropubs?

If you are in Budapest to stay for a while, this book will help you to get to know the city intimately. But it also makes for an interesting read when you are looking to enhance your weekend city trip: just spend some time in one of the book shops, visit one of the art cinemas, and of course, don't forget the artisan beer halls.

THE AUTHOR

András Török was born and raised in Budapest. He is an author, lecturer and long-time observer of his native city's urban scene. He wrote eight books, including the celebrated *Budapest: A Critical Guide*. It was first published in 1989 and has been reprinted and revised many times since then, and it was included in the list of the Ten Best Guidebooks Ever Written by Taras Grescoe.

András Török has worked as a teacher, a typographer and as the deputy minister for culture. He currently is the director of an Arts & Business foundation. As such he works on different projects; his two favourites are the monthly print magazine *Budapest* and the free online photo archive *Fortepan*. He also writes columns, under the name 'Simplicissimus'. Another one of András Török's interests, ever since his student days, is photography. He was the founding director of the Hungarian House of Photography, and he is an active photographer: all the images in this book are his work.

In drawing up his lists the author relied on Budapest's incredibly rich blogosphere; his most trusted sources are *varosban.blog.hu* (by Adam Szűcs and Csaba Magyarósi) and the bilingual *welovebudapest.com*. His thanks also goes out to the friends who have inspired most of his ideas about Budapest: Péter Buza, Judit N. Kósa, Ádám Nádasdy, Noémi Saly and Gyula Zeke. Last but not least the author is indebted to his youngest daughter Emma, who was his in-house assistant during this process.

HOW TO USE THIS BOOK

This guide lists 500 things you need to know about Budapest in 100 different categories. Most of these are places to visit, with practical information to help you find your way. Others are bits of information that help you get to know the city and its habitants. The aim of this guide is to inspire, not to cover the city from A to Z.

The places listed in the guide are given an address, including the neighbourhood, and a number. The neighbourhood and number allow you to find the locations on the maps at the beginning of the book: first look for the map of the corresponding neighbourhood, then look for the right number. Please bear in mind that the names people use for the neighbourhoods in Budapest do not coincide with administrative district boundaries. And another word of caution: these maps are not detailed enough to allow you to find specific locations in the city. You can obtain an excellent map from any tourist office or in most hotels. Or the addresses can be located on a smartphone.

Please also bear in mind that cities change all the time. The chef who hits a high note one day may be uninspiring on the day you happen to visit. The bar considered one of the '5 trendy bars for meeting new people' might be empty on the night you visit. This is obviously a highly personal selection. You might not always agree with it. If you want to leave a comment, recommend a bar or reveal your favourite secret place, please visit the website *www.the500hiddensecrets.com* or follow *@500hiddensecrets* on Instagram or Facebook and leave a comment.

A SHORT INTRO TO BUDAPEST STREET SIGNS

Budapest consists of 23 districts and 203 neighbourhoods. At the top of each and every street sign you'll find the number of the district (always in Roman numerals), its name, and also the name of the neighbourhood within the district. There are some small districts that aren't divided into neighbourhoods; some bigger districts on the other hand have a lot of neighbourhoods. District II. holds the record: it consists of 33 neighbourhoods, most of them going back to the 1840s. Their names were translated from German, the mother tongue of most of the inhabitants in those days.

In the middle of the street sign you'll find the name of the street (or square, lane, road, crescent, etc.), and at the bottom you'll find the street number of the two corner blocks. The arrow also shows you the actual direction of ascension or descension.

In the inner city districts you'll find once pretty, nostalgic wrought iron signs, but some of them are hardly decipherable now. Proper maintenance of these signs is not a forte of the city administration, and it has never been. The more recent standard signs are enamelled, and so more weather-resistant. Occasionally you'll bump into a street sign that's crossed out in red: it shows the earlier name of the street. Law requires to keep on the old sign for at least two years. It helps tourists who arrive with old maps.

Public places in Budapest can bear about three dozen different terms for 'street' or 'square', but it's enough to remember the following, most common three: 'utca' [uh-tsa] = street, 'út' [uh-t] = road, and 'tér' [th-eer] = square.

BUDAPEST

overview

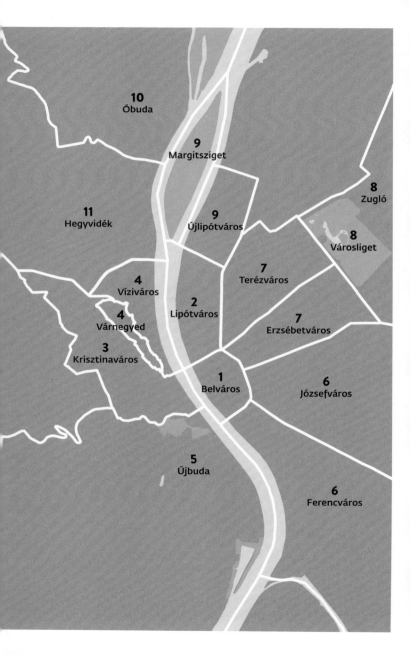

Map 1
BELVÁROS

EAT — DRINK — SHOP — BUILDINGS — DISCOVER — CULTURE — CHILDREN — SLEEP — WEEKEND — RANDO

Map 2
LIPÓTVÁROS

Map 3
KRISZTINAVÁROS

Map 4
VÁRNEGYED and
VÍZIVÁROS

DRINK – SHOP – **BUILDINGS** – DISCOVER – **CULTURE** – CHILDREN – SLEEP – WEEKEND – RANDOM

Map 5
ÚJBUDA

Map 6
JÓZSEFVÁROS *and*
FERENCVÁROS

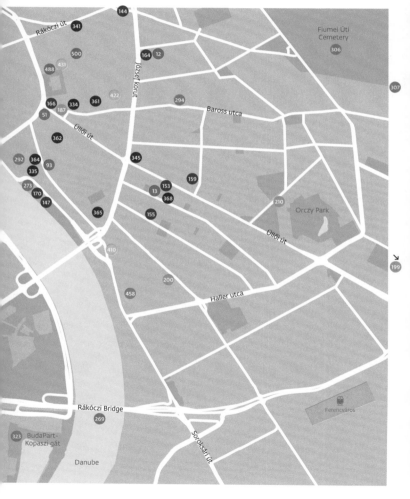

– DRINK – SHOP – BUILDINGS – DISCOVER – CULTURE – CHILDREN – SLEEP – WEEKEND – RANDOM –

Map 7
TERÉZVÁROS and ERZSÉBETVÁROS

Map 8
VÁROSLIGET and
ZUGLÓ

Map 9

MARGITSZIGET *and* **ÚJLIPÓTVÁROS**

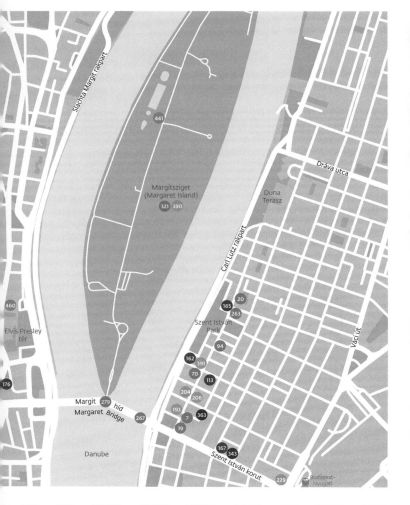

Map 10
ÓBUDA

Map 11
HEGYVIDÉK

95 PLACES TO EAT OR BUY GOOD FOOD

---

5 restaurants to
EAT LIKE A LOCAL

1 **KERÉK VENDÉGLŐ**
III. Bécsi út 103.
Óbuda ⑩
+36 1 250 42 61
kerekvendeglo.hu

This authentic small restaurant in Old Buda with its lovely garden has been in business since the early 1900s – it used to be frequented by the blue-collar workers of a nearby hat factory. The latest facelift took place in 1988. On the menu you'll find grandma's homespun cooking, including two legendary dishes: fried bone marrow with tartar sauce and tripe stew.

2 **CHABLON BISTRO**
VI. Bajcsy-Zsilinszky út 27.
Terézváros ⑦
+36 20 915 7130
chablonbistro.hu

Only regulars and food bloggers know about this no-frills gourmet place tucked away in a courtyard opposite the Arany János utca metro station. The décor is plain, the prices are low, but the menu, which changes weekly, is sophisticated and delicious.

3 **CSALOGATÓ KISVENDÉGLŐ**
XIV. Amerikai út 64.
Zugló ⑧
+36 20 381 4445
csalogato.hu

A popular local institution since the 1930s. These days the 13 tables are often taken by the staff of the film studio and the personel of two hospitals nearby, who come here for lunch; in the evening local families come here for dinner. The pleasant, large terrace can seat about 60 people.

4 FRICI PAPA

VII. Király utca 55.
Erzsébetváros ⑦
+36 1 351 0197
fricipapa.hu

'Uncle Frici' was an instant success when it opened in 1997 and has since then become a Budapest institution. The menu is short and features traditional dishes and low prices. Expect a constant queue on workdays at lunch as well as at dinnertime. Once you get inside, you're free to sit wherever you can find a seat.

5 OPERA HENTES

VI. Hajós utca 21.
Terézváros ⑦
+36 1 353 4022

This butcher's shop overlooks the side of the Opera House; at noon you'll bump into opera stagehands who come here to grab lunch: a fried sausage with mustard and a huge slice of white bread. Among the clientele there are also lawyers and small business owners who are happy to sometimes forget about their healthy, modern diets.

4 FRICI PAPA

The 5 best places for
A HEALTHY MEAL

---

6   **FRUCCOLA**
V. Arany János
utca 32.
Lipótváros ②
+36 1 430 6125
fruccola.hu

This casual and fast self-service restaurant is part of a small chain with two other shops in town. Have a fresh juice made from the fruits of your choice, or compose your own salad. Or try one of the hot dishes on offer; the daily specials are written on the wall. Expect queues, but don't worry, they move surprisingly fast. While waiting you can read a paper or magazine from the great selection, including *Monocle* magazine.

7   **NEMSÜTI VEGA ÉTELBÁR**
XIII. Jászai Mari
tér 4/b.
Újlipótváros ⑨
+36 70 621 1123
+36 70 458 4604
(home delivery)
nemsuti.hu

A great salad bar since 2004. Its name refers to the Hungarian title of a Woody Allen film *(Small Time Crooks)*. You can sit down, or get your order and take it away. Since 2010 there is a home delivery service as well, a rarity as far as salad bars in Budapest go.

8 OH MY GREEN

V. Petőfi Sándor
utca 10.
Belváros ①
+36 1 321 0448
ohmygreen.hu

'Colourful plates, sophisticated flavours. With heart, mind and soul': Oh My Green delivers what their slogan promises. You wouldn't expect such a high-quality place to remain standing in a big shopping street, but thanks to travellers like you Oh My Green manages to do so. Kids are welcome here. Oh My Green also caters to people with different food intolerances and everything is available for takeaway.

9 COYOTE COFFEE & DELI

I. Markovits Iván
utca 4.
Víziváros ④
+36 20 283 6959

Left of the Market Hall on Battyhány tér you'll find this artisan coffeeshop. It's a popular meeting point for friends, colleagues and young couples. It's a small place with limited seating, but you can book a table if you want to be sure to get a taste of those great sandwiches, cakes and cookies.

10 LEGELŐ SALÁTABÁR

VII. Dob utca 46.
Erzsébetváros ⑦
+36 70 949 9997
legelo.net

Legelő – 'pasture' in English – is a small and friendly salad bar loved by people with healthy diets and by strict weight watchers: you can create your own unique salad from a wide range of ingredients and dressings, all of which are listed with their calorie counts and nutrition facts. The focus is on vegetables of course, but there are options for meat eaters as well. Ingredients are sourced locally if possible, and all wrapping materials are fully biodegradable. Open on weekdays only.

5 lesser-known
FOOD MARKETS

---

11 HUNYADI TÉR MARKET

VI. Hunyadi tér 4.
Terézváros ⑦
+36 1 704 2231

This market close to the Grand Boulevard has been serving its densely populated neighbourhood since 1897. Here busy grandmas shop among students, academics and artists. A local pressure group managed to exert influence when the square was redesigned, and thanks to them, the open-air part of the market has remained.

12 RÁKÓCZI TÉR MARKET

VIII. Rákóczi tér 7.
Józsefváros ⑥
+36 1 476 3921

This square used to have a bad reputation as a prostitution area, but cameras put an end to that, and more recently a new station on metro line 4 has accelerated the gentrification of the neighbourhood. The market hall itself was built in 1897 and renovated in 1991 after a fire. The market is open every day, and has an especially good fish selection. Shopping here feels a bit like a social safari.

13 PANCS-GASTROPLACC

ONLY ON SUNDAY

IX. Tűzoltó utca 22.
Ferencváros ⑥
+36 30 921 6286

Young people in Budapest like to go out in what they call 'ruin pubs': pop-up bars, in dilapidated, sometimes roofless buildings that seem ready to be demolished. This ruin pub is one of Budapest's most popular ones, and turns into a community market on Sundays, from 9 am to 2 pm. Up-and-coming and eco-conscious vendors sell artisan delicacies, and visitors are invited to have lunch on the spot.

14 BIOKULTÚRA ÖKOPIAC

ONLY ON SATURDAY
FROM 6.30 AM – 1 PM

XII. Csörsz utca 18.
Hegyvidék ⑪
+36 30 435 5680
biokultura.org/hu/
biokultura-okopiac

This is the Biokultúra Ökopiac market's third location in Buda since its start in 1991. You'll find close to 100 vendors here selling 100% pesticide-free fruit and vegetables, (goat) milk, cheese, jams, juices, and so on. You can also find imported pre-packed bio products and subject-related books. There's a convenient garage for visitors.

15 SZIMPLA KERT FARMERS' MARKET

ONLY ON SUNDAY
FROM 9 AM – 2 PM

VII. Kazinczy utca 14.
Erzsébetváros ⑦
en.szimpla.hu/szimpla-
haztaji/sundaymarket

In 2013 this legendary ruin bar was converted into a split-level community market on Sundays. Between 30 and 40 vendors sell their produce to sometimes up to 2000 visitors. Don't miss the Common Cauldron events, when various NGO's cook the most delicious meals for the visitors using only locally sourced ingredients.

The 5 best places for
SUNDAY BRUNCH

---

16 ARAZ
VII. Dohány
utca 42–44.
Erzsébetváros ⑦
+36 1 815 1100
araz.hu

Araz is 'Zara' spelled backwards, referring to the hotel where this restaurant is located. The building used to be an art nouveau bathhouse; today only the beautiful reception area reminds of that time. The brunch here is probably the best deal in town, considering the variety of food and drinks and the fact that guests of the restaurant can also use the spa facilities free of charge.

17 KIOSK BUDAPEST
V. Március 15. tér 4.
Belváros ①
+36 70 311 1969
kiosk-budapest.com

You could call Kiosk a ruin bar 2.0: it's not really in a ruin, but the interior was inspired by the aesthetics of those typical bars for youngsters. The place is big, offers some wonderful views, and is immaculately run. Also, if you eat here, you're contributing to the maintenance of the Piarist monastery where the restaurant is housed – upstairs there are the chapel and the rooms of the monks.

18 VILLA BAGATELLE

XII. Németvölgyi
út 17.
Hegyvidék ③
+36 30 359 6295 (bistro)
+36 1 213 4191 (bakery)
villa-bagatelle.com

This Buda villa from 1929 was revived in 2010, when a German-Hungarian couple opened a bakery and a cafe here. They set high standards from the beginning and they are still running the business themselves, so you can be assured that those standards are always met. The restaurant and its lovely terrace are a true favourite among the middle-class locals.

19 BUBŌ

XIII. Jászai Mari
tér 3.
Újlipótváros ⑨

Breakfast here is served all day, on the nice (though noisy) terrace, or in the long and narrow inside space. The limited menu features tasty sandwiches and the ambiance is welcoming and family-friendly – on Sundays you'll spot happy couples here, who've left their Macs at home. The kitchen staff is very quick if the place is not too packed. For brunch, be sure to make a reservation.

20 SARKI FŰSZERES

XIII. Pozsonyi
út 53–55.
Újlipótváros ⑨
+36 1 787 7868

The name translates as 'The Corner Grocery Store' but the food here is anything but everyday. From the sandwiches over the meats and cheeses to the wines: everything is of the highest quality. The shop itself is packed with delicacies; seating is on the covered terrace outside, semi-insulated from the street.

5 hip places for
GENERATION-NOW DIETS

---

21 VEGANLOVE

XI. Bartók Béla út 9.
Újbuda ⑤
veganlove.hu

This vegan burger and hot dog place has a great mouth-to-mouth reputation, even among meat-loving locals. Their restaurant is not far from the Buda end of Szabadság Bridge, their food truck can often be spotted at music festivals, and they also have a catering service. A great place for fresh converts to veganism.

22 FREE! THE GLUTEN FREE BAKERY

VII. Dob utca 28.
Erzsébetváros ⑦
+36 30 500 7994
freepekseg.hu

On the ground floor of a block from the 2010s, you'll find this small place and also the almost constant line of people waiting to get in. The tone is set by a black T-shirt on the wall: 'Fuck Gluten!' An amazing variety of special-demand products. A long list of which foods are suitable for which diets is framed on a table for you to study while waiting.

23 CONFECTIONERY NOGLU

II. Fény utca 2.
Országút ③
+36 20 424 0046
noglu.hu

A trendsetter in the health-conscious dessert department since 2010. Here you'll find sweets that are free of anything you might want to avoid. Especially nice is their charity project Matana: customers can recommend a family in need, and NoGlu will send them a cake.

24 SLOW FOODIEZ

VI. Szondi utca 11.
Terézváros ⑦
+36 30 444 1983
slowfoodiez.hu

A small three-level restaurant, just off Grand Boulevard, not far from Western station, serving a wide range of meat-free dishes that will win the hearts of those who are carefully considering eating less meat, and of those who are just curious. The chickpeas omelette and the sweet potato omelette, for example, are remarkably good. You can book a table on their website.

25 NASPOLYA NASSOLDA

VI. Káldy Gyula utca 7.
Terézváros ⑦
+36 70 380 84 07
naspolya.hu

Somewhere between the Opera House and the ruin bars you'll find this unique, innovative pastry shop with a great slogan: 'it is a rawsome place'. And they mean it: all products are made from organic fair trade ingredients and contain no gluten, eggs, dairy, or flour; instead, the focus is on nuts and fruit. Extra points for the effortless, cosy atmosphere.

The 5 best
FOOD SHOPS

---

26 CULINARIS
V. Balassi Bálint
utca 7.
Lipótváros ②
+36 1 373 0028
culinaris.hu

This chic place close to the parliament is by far the best of its kind in Budapest, selling delicacies and speciality ingredients non-foodies might never have heard of. A vast cheese counter, exotic fruits, special teas, frozen fish and prawn, champagne of the most elegant brands… This really is food heaven.

27 DELIZIA GOURMET & MORE
XII. Apor Vilmos
tér 11.
Hegyvidék ⑪
+36 1 951 0204
deliziagourmet.hu

In this large shop in a middle-class neighbourhood shopping centre, the focus is on basic food items with a bio certificate. There's a bistro bar on the spot and cold dishes can be delivered. They also have a catering service.

28 SZÉKELY BOLT

V. Aulich utca 4–6.
Lipótváros ②
+36 70 941 8999
szekelybolt.com

Székely ('Szeklers' in English) are a Hungarian ethnic group originally from the Székelyföld region (Szeklerland) deep in Transylvania, which is now a part of Romania. Szeklers cherish their heritage, including their culinary traditions. Thanks to this shop, which opened in the mid 2010s, Budapest residents can buy all the ingredients they need for typical Szekler dishes. Everything, even dairy, is shipped directly from Szeklerland.

29 CBA PRÍMA CORSO GOURMET

V. Váci utca 54.
Belváros ①
+36 30 428 8376
corsogourmet.hu

This large supermarket is housed in a two-storey building from the 1790s. During the renovation in 2013, a glass extension was built on top of it to make extra room for a restaurant. Despite that cool location, this high-end self-service restaurant tends not to be too crowded; it's a great spot to take a break from sightseeing and enjoy a drink.

30 A NAGYMAMA HÁZI BOLTJA

I. Pauler utca 5.
Krisztinaváros ③
+36 1 202 7393
nagymamaboltja.hu

'Grandma's Grocery' is an eco-friendly family business honouring pre-industrial traditions. They only sell the produce of smallholding farms, and use only recycled wrapping materials. The shop is full of handwritten messages, on a chalkboard and on pieces of paper, which add to the feeling that shopping here makes you part of an eco-conscious community.

The 5 most
ROMANTIC
RESTAURANTS

---

31 BALTAZÁR BUDAPEST

I. Országház utca 31.
Várnegyed ④
+36 1 300 7050
baltazarbudapest.com

For a highly original and innovative culinary experience, this restaurant is the place to be. It's housed in the hotel of the same name, in a peaceful corner of the touristic Castle District. Here you'll enjoy 'gourmet street food' made with ingredients of the highest quality on the charcoal grill that's favoured by chefs like Ramsey and Blumenthal.

32 ARANY KAVIÁR ÉTTEREM

I. Ostrom utca 19.
Várnegyed ④
+36 1 201 6737
aranykaviar.hu

With its theatrical interior this restaurant on the slopes of Castle Hill strives to emanate Czarist splendour. The name means 'Golden caviar' in English and that's no coincidence, because most of the dishes on the extensive menu have caviar in them. Also on the menu are chicken-breast Kyiv style and Stroganoff beefsteak, as well as a nice selection of sea fish. The conservatory is particularly nice.

33 ROBINSON

XIV. Városligeti tó
Zugló ⑧
+36 1 422 0222
robinsonrestaurant.hu

This two-level luxurious place sits on a small island in a pond in the City Park and is as old as Hungary's regained liberty – it opened in 1989. Upstairs you'll find the Tuscan steakhouse, on the ground floor there is the restaurant, serving timeless cuisine. If you get a table on the wonderful terrace, you might bump into some Hollywood celebrity.

34 21 MAGYAR VENDÉGLŐ

I. Fortuna utca 21.
Várnegyed ④
+36 1 202 2113
21restaurant.hu

Regulars know that the name of this restaurant not only refers to the house number but also to 21st-century Hungarian cuisine. The chefs here succeed in what many are trying in Budapest these days: create a lighter, upgraded version of traditional Hungarian food. The vibe here is elegant and informal – as the website says: 'Feel free to talk a little louder'.

35 ÉMILE

II. Orló utca 1.
Hegyvidék ⑪
+36 30 585 0602
emile.hu

In the 19th century the Swiss immigrant pastry-chef Gerbeaud opened a coffee-house in Budapest. In 2014 the owners of this institution took over a second cafe-restaurant in Buda, and gave it Gerbeaud's first name, Émile. In this beautiful villa from the 1920s you'll also find Émile's pastry shop and confectionery. The menu is short but has something for everyone, including kids, who'll definitely enjoy the nice garden.

5 restaurants for
MEAT LOVERS

---

36 KNRDY (AMERICAN STEAKHOUSE & BAR)
V. Október 6. utca 15.
Lipótváros ②
+36 1 788 1685
knrdy.com

This steak restaurant with the name of its owner (pronounced as 'kon-rah-dee'), has the ambition of being the best of its kind in town. The menu features, among other things, dry-aged USDA Prime Black Angus beef, and you can pick the piece of meat you want to eat. The interior has an industrial-romantic feel to it, with a lot of black.

37 HILDA
V. Nádor utca 5.
Lipótváros ②
+36 30 430 9810

The recent large mosaic of a chicken on the wall of this 200-year-old building reveals the speciality of the house: chicken, and duck. The ambiance here is light and pleasant, also thanks to the manners of the staff – you can even observe the chefs while they're cooking. If you want to talk, don't sit near the parrot.

38 MEAT BOUTIQUE
I. Lánchíd utca 7.
Víziváros ④
+36 1 797 9957
meatboutique.hu

A premium-category, meat-based restaurant with a bistro-like informal elegance to it, overlooking Chain Bridge. Everything here feels very contemporary. The menu changes every 4 to 6 weeks.

39 BUJA DISZNÓ(K)

V. Hold utca 13.
(Upstairs at the
market/ shop 6)
Lipótváros ②
+36 70 377 3322

'Lush Pigs' is the most popular of the
dozen or so street food stalls on the
gallery of the Inner City market. Most
people come here for the supersized,
affordable fried pork in breadcrumbs,
served with potato salad – a dish created
by chef Lajos Bíró, of fine dining fame.
Don't come around lunchtime, it gets
super busy then.

40 KISPIAC BISZTRÓ

V. Hold utca 13.
Lipótváros ②
+36 1 269 4231

This traditional neighbourhood
restaurant is located on the right of
the main entrance of the market from
which it gets its name, and practically
all the fresh ingredients for the kitchen.
They can only seat about 20 people inside.
The menu features some permanent
fixtures – Hungarian specialities – as well
as 6 to 8 changing offers.

37 HILDA

The 5 best places for
TRADITIONAL
HUNGARIAN FOOD

---

41 **KÁRPÁTIA**
V. Ferenciek tere 7–8.
Belváros ①
+36 1 317 3596
karpatia.hu

This large, glitzy establishment has been in continuous operation since 1877, and therefore is a rarity in town. The two hallmarks are the traditional Hungarian food – although they are making an effort to serve some lighter, more contemporary dishes as well – and the gypsy music that's played after 6 pm. Don't miss the wall paintings from the 1920s and be sure to taste the wonderful wines and *pálinka* on offer.

42 **MÁRGA BISZTRÓ**
VI. Székely Mihály utca 2.
Terézváros ⑦
+36 70 333 5289

Recently the well-reputed Márga restaurant in Lake Balaton opened this sister establishment in the centre of Budapest, close to the cathedral. As they advertise themselves: a place for 'urban nomads'. The staff know about sophisticated and innovative cooking techniques and buy products like lamb, hare and fish from farmers who share their passion for quality.

43 KÁROLYI ÉTTEREM ÉS KÁVÉHÁZ

V. Károlyi utca 16.
Belváros ①
+36 1 328 0240
karolyietterem.hu

In the historic centre of Pest you'll find a former aristocratic palace that now houses the Petőfi Museum of Literature and this restaurant – truly a hidden secret for tourists. The food is very traditional (Hungarian); think roast goose leg with braised red cabbage and the like. In the summer it's lovely to sit in the garden, under old chestnut trees.

44 ÉS BISZTRÓ

V. Deák Ferenc
utca 12–14.
Lipótváros ①
+36 1 429 3990
esbisztro.hu

The ground floor of the five-star Kempinski Hotel is an unlikely place for a casual Hungarian-Viennese bistro and steakhouse, yet this is where you'll find ÉS. The name stands for 'and': steak and burger, stew and *Wiener schnitzel*, salads and crispy pancetta. But also traditional and innovative: this is Hungarian cuisine at its best.

45 VAKVARJÚ RESTAURANT

VI. Paulay Ede utca 7.
Terézváros ⑦
+36 1 268 0888
pest.vakvarju.com

The name translates as 'Blind Raven' but a *vakvarjú* is also a crunchy edged flatbread from the oven, with goodies on top of it. A big, split level hall, there is a Madame Tussaud style scene on a gallery: the janitor and his wife look down on the bustle. The menu is long, the portions are large and children will love the play corner.

5 great places to eat on
A SMALL BUDGET

---

46 KÁDÁR ÉTKEZDE
VII. Klauzál tér 9.
Erzsébetváros ⑦
+36 1 321 3622

The tiny place is about 60 years old and was named after Mr Kádár. He passed away a long time ago, so now someone else is running the show, but you can still taste the flavours of the 1970s here – mostly working class classics, plus *cholent* only on Saturday. You sit at communal tables, next to people you don't know, which adds to the charm.

47 PASTA.
V. Kálvin tér 2.
Belváros ①
+36 30 241 7760

An eccentric, affordable pasta place, with four daily-changing pastas on offer. You can eat at tables in front of the shop, or in the nearby museum gardens. The dishes have fancy names, like Fat Boy (named after the first A-bomb), Momofuku or Snow White.

48 IGEN
VII. Madách Imre út 5.
Erzsébetváros ⑦
+36 70 355 3054

On the menu: eight monthly-changing kinds of Naples-style thin pizza that can be ordered by the slice. They're baked in a handmade wood oven at 450°, so the pizza is ready in 60 seconds. Be prepared to queue, both outside and inside.

49 GYROS KERKYRA GÖRÖG ÉTELBÁR

VI. Eötvös utca 5.
Terézváros ⑦
+36 70 388 8120
kerkyra.co.hu

This authentic Greek salad bar in a market hall is the place to be for gyros, souvlaki, moussaka, horiatiki, and grills (and they offer some nice sweet treats as well). The website shows photos of all the dishes, together with info on how things are prepared. We love the openness and the hospitality of the staff here, and how clean everything is.

50 TÖLTŐ

VII. Wesselényi utca 31.
Erzsébetváros ⑦
tolto.net

This lovely small sausage bar is called 'Filler'. The young owners fill the raw sausages themselves, and they love to experiment with new flavours. How about a wild boar sausage with shitake mushroom for example, or a chicken sausage with lime and ginger? The beers on the menu have promising names like 'Flying Rabbit' or 'Dark Jerk'.

48 IGEN

The 5 best places for
FINE DINING

---

51 COSTES

IX. Ráday utca 4.
Ferencváros ⑥
+36 1 219 0696
costes.hu

In 2010 this restaurant was the first in Hungary to be awarded a Michelin star. The chef lets international food trends blend perfectly with classic Hungarian cuisine. Most of the ingredients come from Hungarian farms, as well as from the Rungis market in Paris. Try the five-course degustation menu with wine pairing.

52 ONYX RESTAURANT

V. Vörösmarty
tér 7–8.
Belváros ①
+36 30 508 0622
onyxrestaurant.hu

In the centre of Pest you'll find this Michelin-starred restaurant that stands for tradition without being afraid of evolution. In the evening you can either order the six-course Hungarian Evolution menu or the eight-course Chef menu. Fortunately, the décor has evolved as well – the TV screens have disappeared.

53 BABEL

V. Piarista köz 2.
Belváros ①
+36 70 600 0800
babel-budapest.hu

You could describe the cuisine here as avant-garde, the Hungarian-Transylvanian way. Experimentation is the rule: the kitchen staff combine the most unexpected raw ingredients, 75% of which come from Hungary. The knowledgeable waiters and the Scandinavian-like interior are two other reasons to call this place outstanding.

54 FAUSTO'S

VII. Dohány utca 3.
Erzsébetváros ⑦
+36 30 589 1813
fausto.hu

Chef Fausto di Vora opened his restaurant in 1991, together with his Hungarian wife. In fact, it's two-restaurants-in-one: a fine-dining restaurant to the right, and an osteria to the left, with the kitchen in the middle. Most of the products come from Italy, and the owner makes his own olive oil and wine. Don't forget to order some zabaglione or tiramisu for dessert!

55 OLIMPIA VENDÉGLŐ

VII. Alpár utca 5.
Erzsébetváros ⑦
+36 1 321 0680
olimpiavendeglo.com

It may seem hard to believe, but this basement space is Budapest's temple of slow food. There's room for only 13 people, who are expected at 7 pm for an evening-filling programme. There's no menu card, just a list of ingredients on a chalkboard. You decide how many courses you want – four to seven – and then just trust the chefs.

5

INFORMAL GOURMET RESTAURANTS

56 CAFÉ KÖR

V. Sas utca 17.
Lipótváros ②
+36 1 311 0053
cafekor.net

This is a favourite among the businessmen and diplomats who work at the nearby National Bank and the US Embassy, and thus the scene of 'power lunches' at noon. The restaurant feels like a 100-year-old institution, but don't be fooled, it's not. The menu features international food with a Hungarian twist.

57 MÁK BISZTRÓ

V. Vigyázó Ferenc utca 4.
Lipótváros ②
+36 30 723 9383
mak.hu

This design bistro-style restaurant stands out from the other restaurants in the area of the Chain bridge, thanks to the food that's served and the clientele it attracts: busy businessmen, well-to-do couples and bigger groups enjoying the six-course degustation menu. It is worth listening to the great sommelier.

58 BOCK BISZTRÓ

VII. Erzsébet körút 43–49.
Erzsébetváros ⑦
+36 1 321 0340
bockbisztro.hu

In a somewhat glitzy hotel on Grand Boulevard, you'll find this bistro/wine shop, run by maverick chef Lajos Bíró. He loves to fill the chalkboards with special offers and he loves experimenting and shocking regulars. He's a dedicated advocate of informal dinners.

59 LIBERTÉ BUDAPEST

V. Aulich utca 8.
Lipótváros ②
+36 30 715 4635
libertebudapest.com

A chic, original place, with a pleasant terrace to sit from spring to autumn. After rough times during the Communist era, it reopened in the early 2000s, and has had a second makeover since then. It's now sort of a symbol of the new, contemporary Budapest. Downstairs you'll spot staff members of the nearby banks and the US Embassy having their power lunches, upstairs you'll find a pool table.

60 KLASSZ ÉTTEREM ÉS BORBOLT

VI. Andrássy út 41.
Terézváros ⑦
+36 1 599 9490
klasszetterem.hu

A highly popular, easy-going bistro, almost opposite the Opera House, with a limited menu featuring Hungarian and Mediterranean dishes. The place is famous for its ever-changing, imaginative soups, served from copper casseroles. The kitchen is upstairs – the chef looks down on the guests through a large window – and there's a large wine shop in the back. No reservations.

59 LIBERTÉ BUDAPEST

5 places for
JEWISH FOOD

61 KŐLEVES VENDÉGLŐ
VII. Kazinczy utca 41.
Erzsébetváros ⑦
+36 1 322 1011
kolevesvendeglo.hu

'Stone Soup' is a trendy restaurant near the ruin bar area, in a building that used to house a Jewish butcher's. The interior is decorated with old paraphernalia, the cuisine is Hungarian with a modern touch and the friendly student waiters speak English. Upstairs there's a space for events.

62 CARMEL
VII. Kazinczy utca 31.
Erzsébetváros ⑦
+36 1 322 1834
carmel.hu

This split-level, highly traditional, so-called *glatt kosher* restaurant – meaning that the food they serve meets the strictest religious prescriptions – is right in the middle of the Jewish Quarter, next to the orthodox synagogue. There's seating for no less than 100 guests, thanks to the three private rooms.

63 MACESZ BISTRO
VII. Dob Utca 26.
Erzsébetváros ⑦
+36 1 787 6164
maceszbistro.hu

This place attracts an artistic and academic crowd, who love to bring their international friends here to taste the light and modern take on traditional Jewish courses. There are two kinds of degustation menus, which is unusual in this kind of restaurant, and an excellent wine selection.

64 ROSENSTEIN RESTAURANT

VIII. Mosonyi utca 3.
Józsefváros ⑦
+36 1 333 3492
rosenstein.hu

This family-run place grew out of a sausage bar near the Eastern station and became the most renowned Jewish-Hungarian restaurant in Budapest. The food here comes in large portions and is made from ingredients that are produced in an ecological farm. The founder didn't really care about kosher or not: "Everything is kosher that tastes good."

65 SPINOZA HÁZ

VII. Dob utca 15.
Erzsébetváros ⑦
+36 1 413 7488
spinozahaz.hu

This cosy Hungarian-Jewish restaurant was established in 2001 by a Hungarian woman who worked as an economist in Amsterdam before moving back to Budapest to realise her dream. On Fridays musicians play klezmer music during dinner, on other nights there is live piano music. There's also a tiny theatre, but plays are only in Hungarian.

61 KŐLEVES VENDÉGLŐ

5 lovely and small
NEIGHBOURHOOD RESTAURANTS

---

66 MILLENNIUM DA PIPPO

VI. Andrássy út 76.
Terézváros ⑦
+36 1 374 0880
millenniumdapippo.hu

The name of this restaurant refers to the Hungarian Millennium of 1896, when the underground metro line was built, and to Pippo, the Syracuse-born cook who owns this place. The walls resemble those of the metro stations, but perhaps the most striking element in the interior is the classic ham slicer in the hall.

67 FÖLDES JÓZSI VENDÉGLŐJE

III. Bécsi út 31.
Óbuda ⑩
+36 70 500 0222
*foldes-jozsi-vendegloje.
business.site*

Dining here is like travelling back in time. The eponymous cook is gone, but still this restaurant retains the flavours of decades ago. Why? Because the patrons don't want change. Be prepared to queue and try to recognise the celebrities on the wall.

68 'M'

VII. Kertész utca 48.
Erzsébetváros ⑦
+36 31 783 0161
metterem.hu

This place near the Music Academy is a favourite among academics, eccentric artists and former dissidents. Owner Miklos Sulyok was a dissident himself and he still likes to do things differently. He backs up his daughter Janka, who now runs 'M'.

69 ALMÁSY VENDÉGLŐ

II. Rómer Flóris
utca 12.
Hegyvidék ⑪
+36 1 315 1338
almasyvendeglo.hu

This small restaurant is run by the descendants of the Almásy counts – hence the name. This famous Hungarian line of noblemen can be traced back to 1677; the photos on the wall are testimonies of their lives. The restaurant stands for tradition at a high level: as if Communism never happened in Hungary. It's only open for lunch, but groups of six or more can book a table for dinner as well.

70 POZSONYI KISVENDÉGLŐ

XIII. Radnóti Miklós
utca 38.
Újlipótváros ⑨
+36 1 787 4877

Located on the main street of a chic, planned neighbourhood from the late 1930s, this place (with two floors) is always packed at noon. It stands for traditional Hungarian fare and caters to left-leaning or liberal people, who don't care about their weight too much. Lots of guests here seem to bump into people they know sitting at the next table.

The 5 restaurants to go for
GOULASH

---

71 GETTÓ GULYÁS
VII. Wesselényi
utca 18.
Erzsébetváros ⑦
+36 20 376 4480

Where? In the neighbourhood where
once the ghetto was, created by the Nazis
in 1944. What? Gulyás and related foods,
in a great variety. Goulash used to be
called 'the gravedigger of fine dining',
since it is informal and affordable and yet
prepared with care. It's the quintessential
Hungarian family table dish, from
grandma's times.

72 MANDRAGÓRA KÁVÉHÁZ
II. Kacsa utca 22.
Víziváros ④
+36 1 202 2165
mandragorakavehaz.hu

One of inner Buda's best-kept secrets: this
club-like cafe that slowly developed into
a bistro with very attentive service. They
insist on working with farmers they know
and give credit to all of them on the often-
changing menu card, with goulash as the
most popular item on it.

73 KÉHLI VENDÉGLŐ

III. Mókus utca 22.
Óbuda ⑲
+36 1 368 0613
kehli.hu

A traditional Old Buda restaurant, since 1899. A large place, with an extensive menu, with two kinds of goulash: one is the small portion, served in a cup, the other is served in a small, red pot. If you order the latter, you might not want anything else. Try to book a table far away from the gypsy band.

74 RÉZKAKAS BISTRO

V. Sas utca 3.
Lipótváros ②
+36 1 267 0349
rezkakasbistro.hu

This elegant, formal, Hungarian-French restaurant is celebrated for its award-winning goulash and for its signature 'Mangalica Duo' dish of grilled pork with foie gras and Agata potato strudel. It takes about 20 hours to prepare, including 16 hours of sous-vide cooking. There is live gypsy music on most nights.

75 REGŐS VENDÉGLŐ

VI. Szófia utca 33.
Terézváros ⑦
+36 30 944 9375
regosvendeglo.hu

Probably the most traditional Hungarian place of all, in an undistinguished Theresa Town basement. It wasn't on the foodie map, until an undercover *New York Times* critic found it and praised the hell out of it. Great goulash, majestic portions, sincerely affordable.

5 *iconic*
HUNGARIAN
SWEETS

---

76 TÚRÓ RUDI

This curd snack – something between a dairy product and a dessert – has been popular since 1968. It is composed of a thin chocolate-flavoured outer coating and an inner filling of *túró* (curd). There are many varieties, but the one with the polka dots wrap is the best.

77 DOBOS CAKE

A five-layer sponge cake layered with chocolate buttercream and topped with caramel. The pastry is named after Hungarian confectioner József C. Dobos, who created it in 1885 for a National Exhibition. King Franz Joseph was the first to taste it. Nowadays, the recipe has about a hundred varieties.

78 KÜRTŐS KALÁCS

A spit cake originating in the Middle Ages, made from sweet, raised dough, of which a strip is spun and then wrapped around a truncate cone-shaped baking spit, and rolled in granulated sugar. It is roasted over charcoal, until it has a shiny, crispy crust. Nowadays a street food.

79 KAKAÓS CSIGA

These 'cocoa snails' are similar to cinnamon rolls, but with less cinnamon and a lot of melted chocolate. All Hungarian grandmas can make perfect snails, even if they don't remember the exact amounts of ingredients. Now most families buy these from bakeries, to remember the good old days.

80 SZALONCUKOR

Hungarians eat a kilo and a half of 'parlour candy' per household, all before, during and after Christmas. It is usually made of fondant covered with chocolate and wrapped in shiny coloured foil, and then hung on the Christmas tree as a decoration.

76 TÚRÓ RUDI

The 5 best
PASTRY SHOPS

---

81 CAFÉ GERBEAUD

V. Vörösmarty
tér 7–8.
Lipótváros ①
+36 1 429 9000
gerbeaud.hu

The oldest (since 1858) and glitziest pastry shop in town is no secret, but do go inside and have a look. There are three kinds of tables and a lovely, fitting painting by a French master called *The Altar Boy and the Apprentice Confectioner*. Buy some traditional chocolates in designer wrapping – they're really good.

82 DESSZERT.NEKED

VI. Paulay Ede
utca 17.
Terézváros ⑦
+36 20 253 1519
desszertneked.hu

Not far from the Opera House you'll find this high-end pastry shop, where you can buy the most wonderful creations of French and Hungarian desserts. You can also attend workshops to learn how to make their delicacies.

83 MARANGONA

II. Bimbó út 2.
Hegyvidék ④
+36 1 315 0058
marangona.hu

At the entrance of Rose Hill, the most expensive residential area of inner Buda, you'll find this shop that calls itself 'the most girlish place in town'. The workshop specialises in wedding cakes and they are prepared to engage into insane efforts for the great day.

84 ZAZZI CUKRÁSZDA ÉS KÁVÉZÓ

III. Bécsi út 57–61.
Óbuda ⑩
+36 1 240 0688
zazzi.hu

This shop was founded by two ladies; one of them holds a degree in humanities from the Sorbonne, the other is a retired otorhinolaryngologist. They specialise in French delicacies, like *macarons* and fruit, chocolate and caramel mousses. They offer their super-complicated cakes in one-person-portions, so you can first taste before maybe ordering a bigger version.

85 AUGUSZT BELVÁROS

V. Kossuth Lajos
utca 14–16.
Belváros ①
+36 1 337 6379
auguszcukraszda.hu

Auguszt Belváros belongs to a confectioner dynasty of Budapest. The first shop opened in 1870; these days the fifth generation operates three shops. This cosy inner city shop looks as if it has been there since day one, but don't be fooled: it was opened in 2009. The hallmark cake is 'the E-80', created for the 80th birthday of Elemér Auguszt.

85 AUGUSZT BELVÁROS

5 *tempting*
ICE-CREAM PARLOURS

---

86 **ARTIGIANA GELATI**
XII. Csaba utca 8.
Hegyvidék ③
+36 1 212 2439

This was the first place to serve decent Italian ice cream in Budapest, in 1990. There are more than 40 flavours and the quality is always top-notch. Favourites are the pistachio, dark chocolate and cheesecake ice cream and also the lemon and pear flavours. There are options for lactose sensitive customers as well.

87 **VALDOCCO**
V. Múzeum körút 7.
Belváros ①
+36 1 318 6717

The name refers to the Torino suburb where the Salezian Order was founded. Mr Rüzsics, the owner, is a great supporter of that order, and that's why this ice-cream parlour is the only one in Budapest where you'll see a cross hanging on the wall. He offers about 50 varieties, the portions are super large.

88 **MORITZ EIS**
V. Dorottya utca 6.
Belváros ①
+36 30 307 7163
moritzeis.com

This premium ice-cream parlour is part of a Serbian-owned global business. You can trust the names of the different flavours: the raw ingredients really come from the place stated on the label. In 2017 they moved to the place where they belong: the inner city. Open till 11 pm.

89 GELARTO ROSA

V. Szent István tér 3.
Lipótváros ②
+36 70 383 1071
gelartorosa.com

This shop is no secret: just look for the winding queue of ice-cream lovers in front of it. They love the rose-shaped presentation, but also the no-compromise approach when it comes to selecting ingredients, staff and technology. The place was launched by a lady with tons of energy, with the support of her French gourmet husband. They also run a small bistro nearby.

90 ERDŐS ÉS FIAI

XI. Etele tér 3.
Újbuda ⑤
+36 1 203 3226
erdosesfiai.hu

'Erdos and Sons' is located near Kelenföld station, away from the city centre. Norbert Erdős speaks Italian: he fell in love with gelati while working in Italy. It took him two decades to find the courage to open his own shop, designed by his wife. Their sons were too young then, but were nevertheless included in the name. Try the alcohol-flavoured varieties.

89 GELARTO ROSA

5 *not-to-miss*
ARTISAN BAKERS

---

91 JACQUES LISZT

V. Apáczai Csere
János utca 7.
Belváros ①
+36 30 506 5968

The master baker who runs this artisan bakery used to work as a lawyer in a bank, and then turned his life around under the spell of a TV-programme. After closing time you can see the bakers at work, making all the bread and pastries from additive-free ingredients. The name Jacques Liszt in Hungarian means 'a sack of flower'.

92 ARTIZÁN BAKERY BUDAPEST

V. Hold utca 3.
Lipótváros ②
+36 30 856 5122
artizan.hu

For Gergő Fekete it all started with a blog (in English) about his hobby – baking. Now he runs a lovely and busy split-level bakery and cafe, where everything is prepared on the spot. You'll find some of the tastiest sandwiches in town here, and good coffee made with their own beans.

93 BUTTER BROTHERS

IX. Lónyay utca 22.
Ferencváros ⑥
+36 30 456 4019
butter-brothers.com

A lovely breakfast place and bakery in one, very close to the Central Market. On offer: among other things, a variety of pastries, excellent coffee, and some craft beers. At lunch time they serve a daily soup with sandwiches, and all day long you can order super fresh milk from the owner's very own cows.

94 HÁROM TARKA MACSKA

XIII. Pozsonyi út 41.
Újlipótváros ⑨
+36 1 785 7892

'Three Mottled Cats' is a busy artisan bakery on the corner of a street in the middle-class neighbourhood New Leopold Town. It opened in 2017, and was an instant success, even though there are lots of other bakeries nearby. On weekend mornings it's very hard to find a spot to sit and eat a sandwich because it's so crowded, but at any other time this is a peaceful place with a nice décor.

95 BRÓT

AT: VILLA BAGATELLE
Németvölgyi út 17.
Hegyvidék ③
+36 1 213 4191
villa-bagatelle.com/hu/
brotpekseg

This nice cafe is housed in a villa from the 1920s, with a bakery on the ground floor. It used to be a red lamp house in the 1990s. The place was renovated and is now run by a German-Hungarian couple, who personally watch over the quality of their goods. Everything is made by hand here, without the use of unnatural additives.

94 HÁROM TARKA MACSKA

KUPLUNG

85 PLACES TO GO FOR A DRINK OR PARTY

5 of the
COOLEST BARS

---

96 LA BODEGUITA DEL MEDIO

VII. Dob utca 57.
Erzsébetváros ⑦
+36 20 388 2738
labodeguitadelmedio.hu

This legendary venue was built in 1901 for an association of artists, actors, writers and architects called 'The Nest'. It survived communist times and now operates as a Cuban-style place, with an orchestra called La Movida. It's unlike any other place in Budapest, and should not be missed by lovers of Caribbean vibes and drinks.

97 TUK TUK BAR

VI. Paulay Ede utca 31.
Terézváros ⑦
+36 1 343 1198
tuktukbar.hu

In a street off busy Andrássy út you'll find this nostalgic-feeling bar. The décor and the spices in the drinks (coriander, basil, chilli, ginger, lemongrass and lemon): everything here is inspired by the Shanghai of the 1920s. Once a week, there is live jazz. Most cocktails have names and stories related to the award-winning barmen.

98 WARM UP

VII. Nagy Diófa utca 26.
Erzsébetváros ⑦
+36 70 534 0012
warmupbudapest.hu

Unlike in other bars you won't find a long drink list here, in fact there's no list at all. Talk a bit to the bartender, about your preferences, and he creates your personal cocktail, under your very eyes. No two cocktails are exactly alike here.

99 BAR PHARMA
**VII. Kazinczy
utca 35.
Erzsébetváros ⑦
+36 30 294 3177
barpharma.hu

This very small bar (with only ten stools) reminds passers-by of a pharmacy: there are bottles and other, smaller glass containers, and plants are hanging from the ceiling. The atmosphere is very different from the usual pub or ruin bar feeling. They have exotic cocktails of their own making, like the pho-based one or the one named after the bar.

100 BOUTIQ'BAR
**VI. Paulay Ede
utca 5.
Terézváros ⑦
+36 30 554 2323
boutiqbar.hu

This bar opened in 2008, a month before the crisis hit Hungary, and it barely survived at first. But then their luck changed: they were elected best bar in Hungary, and in 2012 they were named one of the 50 best bars in the world. They are strong in whiskies and bourbons (you can even taste a Japanese variety), whereas the choices in wine or beer are limited.

97 TUK TUK BAR

5 great

HUNGARIAN ALCOHOLIC BEVERAGES

101 UNICUM

A dry bitter, made according to a secret recipe with over 40 herbs, and mostly drunk as an aperitif. When the emperor Joseph II tried it in 1790 he allegedly said: "Das ist ein Unicum!" – hence the name. Its unmistakable bottle has the shape of a globe and has a red cross on it. The drink is produced by the Zwack family, who also have a lovely small museum.

102 PÁLINKA

This is the name of the traditional Hungarian fruit brandy. The varieties made from plums, apricots, apples, pears, and cherries are best known, but there's also a walnut version and many more. Pálinka has been produced and drunk in Hungary since the Middle Ages. Look for small, emerging labels.

103 TOKAJ WINES
WHITE WINE

The Tokaj wine region in North-East Hungary attracted a lot of French investors in the 1990s. They restored the region's old glory. Earlier the region was mostly renowned for its sweet dessert wine called Aszú, lately the dry varieties have taken the upper hand. It's worth visiting the region and staying overnight; the wineries offer accommodation too.

104 TÖRLEY
SPARKLING WINE

József Törley established his factory in 1882, in a suburb called Budafok. After a less than glorious communist period, the company is booming again, after merging with other Hungarian brands. It produces over 21 million bottles of sparkling wine a year. Budapest people still call it champagne, even though the EU decided that this name can't be used for wines produced outside the French Champagne region.

105 DREHER CLASSIC
BEER

District X., or Kőbánya, became the home of the beer industry thanks to Antal Dreher Jr., son of the founder of the Dreher brewery. Under his leadership the brewery became market leader in the 1870s. During communist times the name was changed to Kőbányai. Since 1990 the modernised factory has changed owners several times. Currently it is in the hands of a Japanese company; luckily the beer still tastes great.

5 of the best
WINE BARS

---

106 ST. ANDREA WINE & GOURMET BAR

V. Bajcsy-Zsilinszky út 78.
Lipótváros ②
+36 1 269 0130
standreaborbar.hu

St. Andrea is the label of a fast-growing winegrower from the area around the small historic town of Eger in North-East Hungary. The label was named after the winegrower's wife. Their elegant, somewhat over-designed wine bar only serves their own wines, both white and red ones. It's on the corner of a former printing house that was converted into an office block.

107 DIVINO BAZILIKA

V. Szent István tér 3.
Lipótváros ②
+36 70 935 3980
divinoborbar.hu

The list here features 140 wines for you to taste, including wines produced by the second generation of great Hungarian winegrowers and off-the-beaten-path labels. They serve some food, too: goose delicacies, beef carpaccio, prawns and other small bites, and some vegetarian options as well.

108 PALACK BORBÁR

XI. Szent Gellért
tér 3.
Újbuda ⑤
+36 30 997 1902
palackborbar.hu

Located in a rapidly gentrifying area, this bar is a meeting point for students and staff of the nearby Technical University, and people visiting the art galleries. It's a remarkably easy-going, friendly place, with absolutely no wine snobbery. The rich wine list is categorised by type, not by region, which is great for beginners.

109 KADARKA

VI. Király utca 42.
Terézváros ⑦
+36 1 266 5094
kadarkabar.hu

This independent wine bar is meant to surprise even the connoisseurs: the list features many small-scale and never-heard-of labels and the atmosphere is very pleasant, despite the location on the main street of a nightlife district. The food is simple – mostly dips, chips and tapas. This is the bar where drinking spritzers isn't considered rude, it's even encouraged.

110 DOBLO

VII. Dob utca 20.
Erzsébetváros ⑦
+36 20 398 8863
budapestwine.com

In this nightlife (and ruin bar) neighbourhood more and more places are emerging with names that are a combination of street names. This one is on the corner of Dob utca and Holló utca, hence Dobló. The interior is a cross between that of a contemporary cafe and a typical wine cellar. There's a 13-metre-long counter to ensure parallel service.

The 5 best places for
A GOOD CUP OF COFFEE

---

111 ESPRESSO EMBASSY

V. Arany János
utca 15.
Lipótváros ②
+36 20 445 0063
espressoembassy.hu

This hip cafe offers high-quality coffee, made from Has Bean beans by award-winning baristas operating La Marzocco machines. The interior features bare brick walls and designer lamps made out of gas pipes. Popular among locals who come here to work on their MacBooks. Obviously they love what they are served.

112 MADAL ESPRESSO & BREW BAR

V. Alkotmány utca 4.
Lipótváros ②
+36 70 270 2559
madalcafe.hu

This big cafe near the parliament building opened in 2017. Apart from great coffee, they strive to offer a peaceful retreat in the urban jungle. The name comes from the peace philosopher Sri Chinmoy (1931–2007), whom the owners feel inspired by – 'Madal' was his nickname as a child. Light, wood-based furniture, pasta-based food at lunchtime.

113 DOUBLE SHOT

XIII. Pozsonyi út 16.
Újlipótváros ⑨
+36 70 249 2665

'We don't like bad coffee, that's why we opened', says the inscription on the door. This tiny shop with an upstairs seating area opens at 7 in the morning. It's also a good place for breakfast. A coffee shop with a very complex personality.

114 MY LITTLE MELBOURNE

VII. Madách Imre út 3.
Erzsébetváros ⑦
+36 70 394 7002
mylittlemelbourne.hu

These tiny twin shops are the result of barista experience brought from Melbourne to Budapest. One shop offers machine-made coffee, the other one filter coffee. They also import and roast coffee beans and they train baristas. All in all: they are crusaders for better coffee in Budapest. Apart from coffee, they serve tea, juices, cakes and sandwiches.

115 KELET CAFÉ AND GALLERY

XI. Bartók Béla út 29.
Újbuda ⑤
+36 20 456 5507

This cafe was founded by a geography teacher and a sociologist, and calls itself 'a quality-oriented coffee shop, a used book exchange point and an art gallery'. There are thousands of books and you can take whichever one you like if you replace it by another one you have brought from home. The interior is anti-industrial: clumsy and old-fashioned, a bit like the home of a bachelor academic.

112 MADAL ESPRESSO & BREW BAR

5 trendy cafes for
MEETING NEW PEOPLE

---

116 CAFÉ ZSIVÁGÓ
VI. Paulay Ede
utca 55.
Terézváros ⑦
+36 30 212 8125
cafezsivago.hu

One of the owners has Russian ancestors, hence the name, and the vibe: it feels like stepping onto a seventies film set of *War and Peace*. On the menu: all kinds of drinks, nice teas and a dozen snacks. The number one item on it is the 'homemade *pirog* straight from Tatyana's oven' – you should try it. There's a nice boudoir-like space upstairs. Occasionally there is live music.

117 BÖRZE
V. Nádor utca 23.
Lipótváros ②
+36 1 426 5460
borzeetterem.hu

'Exchange' was the most promising newcomer on the gastro scene in 2017. It took ten years of planning, building and preparing before this place finally opened. It turned out to be a cross between a bistro restaurant, a cafe and a shop and became popular overnight thanks to the very affordable lunch menu and the insanely smooth service. The interior is dominated by a lot of (probably a bit too much) brass. Open daily from 7.30 am to midnight.

118 CAFÉ PONYVAREGÉNY

XI. Bercsényi utca 5.
Újbuda ⑤
+36 30 920 2470
cafeponyvaregeny.hu

The name of Café 'Pulp Fiction' refers to the film, incredibly popular among the students of the Budapest Institute of Technology campus nearby. It is in a large, cosy basement with early 20th-century furniture, books and board games, where people can enjoy coffee, food and cakes and are encouraged to stay and work or to talk to each other. This second venue near the Kopaszi gát park is bigger and super child-friendly.

119 CAT CAFÉ

VI. Révay utca 3.
Terézváros ⑦
+36 20 617 3301
catcafebudapest.hu

No, this isn't a place where you can bring your cats; it's for people who love cats, but for some reason can't have any. At the moment this cafe is the home of ten cats, most of them left behind by their previous owners. On the menu: coffee, tea, cocktails and some cakes. Near Budapest Cathedral.

120 OPERA CAFÉ

VI. Andrássy út 22.
Terézváros ⑦
+36 1 800 9210
operacafe.hu

The Budapest Opera is no secret to tourists, but its cafe is nice, and especially handy if you're meeting up with Budapest acquaintances. It used to be the ticket office, and in those days, you could see long lines of people queuing in front of it, guided by a complicated labyrinth of brass railings to keep order. It's a premium cafe, and prices are according.

The 5 most
BEAUTIFUL CAFES

---

121 CENTRÁL
V. Károlyi utca 9.
Belváros ①
+36 1 266 2110
centralkavehaz.hu

A veritable Grand Café, from 1889. It was closed by the communists in 1949 and reopened in 2000. The cafe part is to the left, the restaurant is to the right, and the pool tables are upstairs. This was the favourite place of many writers, who came here to work because their homes weren't properly lit or heated.

122 HADIK
XI. Bartók Béla út 36.
Újbuda ⑤
+36 1 279 0290
hadik.eu

Another literary cafe, frequented by writers who lived nearby, like comic genius Frigyes Karinthy. These days the large venue operates as two different cafes: Hadik is the more formal space with Thonet chairs, the other (bigger) part is a 'ruin bar version 2.0'-style place: chaotic and colourful.

123 TRANZIT ART CAFÉ
XI. Kosztolányi
Dezső tér /
Baranyai utca
Újbuda ⑤
+36 1 209 3070
tranzitcafe.com

The lovely long-distance bus station was completed in 1963. In 2004 it was converted into a cafe – the signs and the artwork on the wall were all retained. Orsolya Egri, the workaholic owner, has made it into a cafe and community centre, hosting all kinds of art and civic events.

124 NEW YORK CAFÉ

**VII. Erzsébet
körút 9–11.
Erzsébetváros** ⑦
+36 1 886 6167
newyorkcafe.hu

The glitziest Grand Café in town is another literary shrine. It was closed in 1949 and then used as a sportswear store, until it reopened in 1954. In the 1980s the place finally got its name back as well. The walls are the same, but the atmosphere of the early days is gone: the cafe is now part of a luxury hotel, and you have to wait at the entrance to get a seat.

125 CSENDES VINTAGE BAR & CAFÉ

**V. Múzeum körút 13.
Belváros** ①
+36 30 727 2100
csend.es

There used to be a classic cafe here, then for decades there was a small restaurant, frequented by academics and owners of small businesses from the area. In 2008 it reopened as a vintage bar, decorated by some young artists with recycled trash-items. The interior is really intense and colourful, a perfect match for the cold and warm premium drinks that are served. Occasionally live music.

5 *lovely*
ROOFTOPS *and* OTHER TERRACES

---

126 ST. ANDREA WINE & SKYBAR

V. Deák Ferenc
utca 5.
Belváros ①
+36 1 397 9903
standreaskybar.hu

On top of a luxury shopping centre called Váci 1, this all-seasons rooftop bar offers an absolutely unique panorama in every direction. Apart from St. Andrea wines from the Eger region, the drinks list features great spirits, champagnes, spumantes and cocktails. If you're hungry, you can order some gourmet bar food.

127 LÖVŐHÁZ UTCA TERRACES

II. Lövőház utca,
pedestrian section,
between Fény utca
and Káplár utca
Hegyvidék ③④⑪

This street off the Inner Buda junction Széll Kálmán tér used to have lots of traffic, until cars were banned from it in 2010. Almost overnight terraces were installed. There are about a dozen places here, from espresso and cocktail bars to Shakesbeer and Polar Fox (Sarki Róka) pubs, and many more. A great spot to meet up people for drinks.

128 CZAKÓ KERT

I. Czakó utca 15.
Hegyvidék ③
+36 1 501 4002
czakokert.hu

A hardly-known oasis in the Sun Hill part of the inner Buda hills. After opening in the mid 2010s, this garden bistro, terrace and pastry shop became a favourite among young Buda families. There's a market on Saturdays.

129 360 BAR

VI. Andrássy út 39.
Terézváros ⑦
+36 30 356 3047
360bar.hu

The Paris Department Store opened in 1911 and reopened after a renovation in 2009. The rooftop cafe is open from spring to autumn and offers a magical panorama. It's a highly original place, a perfect combination of old and new. It opens at 2 pm, and stays quite deserted until about 5. Later on it gets very crowded, so a reservation is essential.

130 ARIA HOTEL ROOFTOP TERRACE

V. Hercegprímás utca 5.
Lipótváros ②
+36 1 445 4055
ariahotelbudapest.com

This music-themed boutique hotel (a sister venue of the Library Hotel in New York) has an incredibly high rooftop bar: it's almost as high as the panorama deck of the nearby cathedral. The over-adorned hotel follows an interesting concept: the four wings have different music themes, respectively classical, opera, contemporary and jazz.

126 ST. ANDREA WINE & SKY BAR

5 bars for the
LGBTQ+ COMMUNITY

---

131 WHY NOT CAFÉ

V. Belgrád
rakpart 3–4.
Belváros ①
+36 1 780 4545
whynotcafe.hu

The gay scene in Budapest isn't large and changes a lot. This Pest riverfront cafe has straight clients in the afternoon, but becomes an exclusively gay hangout in the evening. The design got a facelift in 2016, but still: don't expect Berlin standards here. There are live concerts and karaoke, and you can order some light food.

132 HABROLÓ CAFÉ AND BAR

V. Szép utca 1.
Belváros ①
+36 1 950 6644
habrolo.hu

This well-known, centrally-located miniature bar was named after a salty delicacy: a sort of cylinder filled with soft creamy cheese, and always available. Twice a week there are karaoke parties. Despite the size of the place there are bowling parties – on Xbox.

133 ALTEREGO DANCE CLUB

VI. Dessewffy
utca 33.
Terézváros ⑦
+36 70 565 1111
alteregoclub.hu

Not far from the opera, this club is also a place for younger people; if you are over 30, you are considered sort of a senior. A critic called it a 'plush-decorated gay dance club' that 'allows for pleasant cruising and mingling'. You should arrive early if you want to be able to see the small stage – there are some great drag shows.

134 SZOCIÁLIS HELYISÉG (SOCIAL ROOM)

VII. Kazinczy
utca 52/c.
Erzsébetváros ⑦
+36 20 974 0078

Not exclusively gay; rather a gay-friendly gastro pub, with a friendly staff. The name is ironic: it's a generic term in Hungarian to refer to the spaces used by factory workers to change or to eat their modest meals. You'll find this place right in the middle of the party area, half way between Deák tér and Grand Boulevard; still it's relatively calm here.

135 GAY AND LESBIAN DANCE PARTIES

VARYING VENUES

A new and interesting development in the gay scene, especially since the mid 2010s, is the 'travelling party'. You should register to be notified about the venue. Look out for the following ones: !Szkafander, Garcons, Ösztrosokk (Lesbian), WOW! (Women on women), Omoh and Vibe. The parties usually take place in the weekends, some of them only once a month.

The 5 most
AUTHENTIC
RUIN BARS

---

136 SZIMPLA
VII. Kazinczy utca 14.
Erzsébetváros ⑦
+36 20 261 8669
szimpla.hu

When the word 'ruin bar' was thought up back in 2002, it was to describe this bar, housed in a temporarily unused, neglected building. It was launched by business students who didn't have money to invest – hence the flea market and discarded furniture. Today it is still flourishing and it has even become a kind of shrine: the first of its kind, and a prelude of what was to come.

137 ELLÁTÓ KERT
VII. Kazinczy
utca 48.
Erzsébetváros ⑦
+36 20 527 3018

The name of this usually not too crowded pub means 'Provider' – it's a complicated hint to company names of the communist period. The food here (various taco and chicken courses) is better than next door, and the toilets are cleaner.

138 FOGAS
VII. Akácfa
utca 49–51.
Erzsébetváros ⑦
+36 70 638 5040
fogashaz.hu

At the moment this place is the most complex ruin bar in town, bringing four originally separate places together (Fogas, Kert, Liebling, Lärm), with smaller and bigger interconnected spaces, a large dance floor and a garden. In 2017 also Instant moved to this complex. A labyrinth worth discovering.

139 KUPLUNG

VI. Király utca 46.
Terézváros ⑦
+36 30 755 3527

'Gear Box' is housed in a converted former garage, and best known as a late-night music venue. Its often-changing décor still retains an old decoration at the ceiling: a whale out of cardboard and paper. "If you want to have some refreshment or eat something, release stress or put the pedal to the metal, we're awaiting you at Kuplung."

140 ANKER'T

VI. Paulay Ede
utca 33.
Terézváros ⑦
+36 30 360 3389

This is the summer sister venue of Anker Club, with two courtyards and a giant video wall. People come here for the talented alternative DJs and the occasional slam poetry nights. A minimalist design was added to crumbling walls. The food is better than what you usually get in ruin bars.

136 SZIMPLA

The 5 smoothest
NEXT-GENERATION RUIN BARS

---

141 SPÍLER
VI. Király utca 13.
(Gozsdu Arcade)
Terézváros ⑦
+36 1 878 1309
spilerbp.hu

This place was the first newly-created venue to imitate the ruin bar aesthetics. In Hungarian *spíler* means 'cool guy', but in this case it refers to a story from the 1920s, about a womanising champion boxer – you'll see him on posters and photos in the spectacular interior. Sister venue Spíler Shanghai is across the street.

142 MOST CONTEMPORARY BISTRO
VI. Zichy Jenő utca 27.
Terézváros ⑦
+36 70 248 3322
mostbisztro.hu

In Hungarian *most* means 'now'. The bar is housed in a former factory with glass ceilings; it is revamped every now and then. It has a great terrace on top, with a nice view, and two separate, smaller rooms. Hamburgers, Hungarian and international courses, nice brunch menu. Music on Saturdays at noon.

143 MAZEL TOV
VII. Akácfa utca 47.
Erzsébetváros ⑦
+36 70 626 4280
mazeltov.hu

This informal, elegant meeting point, restaurant and event space opened in the summer of 2014 and was an instant success. A perfect blend of old and new. Happy locals and young foreigners come here for the great party food and music.

144 JELEN BISZTRÓ

VIII. Blaha Lujza
tér 1–2.
Józsefváros ⑥
+36 20 344 3155

A plain, large, black-walled room on the back corner of a grand, neglected department store from 1926. The owners merged an existing restaurant and a pub to create an alternative ruin pub, a meeting point of artsy folks. It opens at 9 am, yet they still offer breakfast. Hopefully the pub will survive the imminent facelift of the building.

145 HUMBÁK KLUB

VII. Király utca 43.
Erzsébetváros ⑦
+36 30 340 3834
humbakmuvek.com

This is the pub of a mysterious, obscene blogger, a fictitious, alcoholic priest, a dropout. This 'Father Tibi' (possibly he's three persons in real life) has more than a million followers now. Supposedly he is a pastor in the village the pub was named after. The space is decorated with alcohol-related witticisms from the blog. It serves affordable wines and spritzers.

The 5 bars with the
LONGEST BEER LIST

---

146 CSAKAJÓSÖR
VII. Kertész
utca 42–44.
Erzsébetváros ⑦
+36 1 950 2788
csakajosor.hu

'Only the good beer' is an amazing shop near the Music Academy selling innumerable kinds of beer, from labels from 18 countries. In the shop there are six taps, with beers that aren't available otherwise, for you to taste. They have a home delivery service if you order a minimum of one bottle – a very friendly quantity.

147 JÓNÁS CRAFT BEER HOUSE
AT: BÁLNA CENTRE
IX. Fővám tér 11–12
Ferencváros ⑥
+36 70 930 1392
balnabudapest.hu

Named after the biblical hero, and located in a shopping centre named 'The Whale', on the riverfront. It has a cool, industrial look, an artsy vibe, and a great panorama on the river. Apart from craft beers – they also have their own label – you can taste craft juices and *pálinkas*.

148 LEGFELSŐBB BEERÓSÁG

VII. Dohány utca 20.
Erzsébetváros ⑦
+36 1 790 3191
beerosag.hu

The funny name is a pun: it means 'supreme court', but with the word 'beer' included. It's a relatively small, split-level space, with chalkboards that offer information on the more than 100 labels you can taste. You can even study a tongue-in-cheek 'periodic table' of beer varieties. The chef's selection also consists of beers.

149 LÉHŰTŐ

VII. Holló utca 12–14.
Erzsébetváros ⑦
+36 30 731 0430

This carefully designed, high-ceiling basement is a serious beer place. The name is a pun, it means both 'juice chiller' and 'rascal'. Six taps with a continuously changing offer, plus many bottled varieties – look for the ticks on the chalkboards. Very friendly and knowledgeable staff. Simple, but tasty food, mainly burgers and tapas.

150 MATRÓZ KOCSMA SÖNTÉSE (AKA THE SAILOR TAPROOM)

I. Bem rakpart 15.
Víziváros ④
+36 1 788 6590
sontes.hu

This large Belgian beer bar is next-door to the design hotel called art'otel, on the Buda riverfront. They have about 20 beers on taps, and also offer more than 200 bottled varieties. It's a great place for beginners as well as for connoisseurs. Some simple food is available but only to facilitate more drinking. There's also a great terrace.

151 FIRST CRAFT BEER

5 bars that offer
SMALL-SCALE
BEER LABELS

---

151 FIRST CRAFT BEER

IV. Váci út 83.
Újpest
+36 30 349 6052
firstcraftbeer.com

Be careful when you're looking for this place: the house numbers of Váci út start back from 1 in District IV.; it would cost you a 20-minute taxi drive. This is an open brewery, meaning that you can see everything through windows – the people working and the workshop, which is as clean as a surgical theatre. Eight varieties are offered in the taproom, none of them very strong.

152 HUNYADI LAKÁSBISZTRÓ ÉS KÉZMŰVES SÖRÖZŐ

I. Hunyadi János
utca 15.
Várnegyed ④
+36 70 881 8100
lakasbisztro.hu

This 'apartment bistro and artisanal brewery' is on the slopes of Castle Hill. It takes up the entire ground floor of a 200-year-old block, overlooking a small square. The focus is on beer, but there's also something for wine-lovers. There's a small private room for smaller groups, called the apartment. There are also beer-related events.

153 ÉLESZTŐ CRAFT BEER BAR

IX. Tűzoltó utca 22.
Ferencváros ⑥
+36 70 336 1279
elesztohaz.hu

This large bar was founded by the organisers of a beer event celebrating emerging craft beer labels. They offer 21 craft beers on tap, all high-quality and Hungarian. The bar also functions as a cultural entertainment zone and a venue for beer-related events. Next door to the Trafo centre of contemporary arts.

154 KANDALLÓ ARTISANAL PUB

VII. Kertész utca 33.
Erzsébetváros ⑦
+36 1 788 3568
kandallopub.hu

'Fireplace' inherited its name: the building used to house a fireplace shop. As such, it isn't very centrally located. It's an informal beer-based gastro pub, rather than a beer hall. There are 16 constantly changing beers on tap. The menu features artisan food, made with products from carefully selected partners.

155 PEPIN CRAFT BEER HOUSE

IX. Tompa utca 26/b.
Ferencváros ⑥
+36 20 280 6477
pepin.hu

Uncle Pepin is a character created by Bohumil Hrabal, an incredibly popular and super funny Czech writer who's widely known in Hungary. Apart from beer from one of the three taps and 40 to 60 kinds of bottled beer, they sell every book written by Hrabal as well as other beer-related books and recent publications about literature.

5 *authentic*

CLUBS *or* CLUB-LIKE PLACES

---

156 BRODY STUDIOS
VI. Vörösmarty
utca 38.
Terézváros ⑦
brody.land/brody-studios

A combination of artists' studios and of an English-speaking élite club, part of an international network. The venue takes up three levels of a partially-renovated Theresa Town block from the 1880s, and is a great place for hosting weddings and other events. Food is served only around dinnertime. Ask about their members-only or invitation-only events.

157 AKVÁRIUM KLUB
V. Erzsébet tér 12.
Belváros ②
+36 30 860 3368
akvariumklub.hu

A highly popular venue in the Budapest youth scene, hosting pop concerts under the ground, in a spot where three underground lines meet. It has a remarkable history: the space was meant to be the garage and the lower levels of the New National Theatre, but the construction works were stopped in 1998, and the theatre was built elsewhere. Occasionally conferences take place here.

158 GÖDÖR CLUB

VI. Király utca 8–10.
Terézváros ⑦
+36 20 201 3868
godorklub.hu

A youth club in an inner-city arcade, with an alternative bias. The name 'Pit Club' refers to the abandoned New National Theatre construction site nearby – 'National Pit' was the ironic name of the unfinished project. They also host charity events.

159 THE GRUND

VIII. Nagytemplom utca 30.
Józsefváros ⑥
+36 20 583 6712
agrund.hu

Corvin Quarters is an urban rehabilitation project that started with the demolition of small, poor-quality building blocks. A few of them remained – one of which now houses this little hotel and ruin bar. The name refers to the temporarily vacant building site that was used by teenage boys as a playground in the classic youth novel *The Paul Street Boys*.

160 TOLDI KLUB

V. Bajcsy-Zsilinszky út 36–38.
Lipótváros ②
+36 30 666 3456
toldiklub.hu

This is the foyer of the popular, two-room art cinema downtown. It's the venue of smaller-scale film festivals and award ceremonies, and also a meeting point with an intellectual atmosphere and relatively affordable drinks and simple food. The permanent posters art work at the entrance summarises the stories of some great classic films.

5 welcoming
NEIGHBOURHOOD CAFES

---

161 ANGELIKA
I. Batthyány tér 7.
Víziváros ④
+36 1 225 1653
angelikacafe.hu

This very old-fashioned, thick-walled cafe on the riverfront is the traditional meeting place of the Buda conservative middle class. The customers' hair tends to be silver – they arrive with or without children and grandchildren. They quarrel over cookies in a low voice, so as not to be overheard.

162 CAFÉ PANINI
XIII. Radnóti Miklós utca 45.
Újlipótváros ⑨
+36 70 946 8072
cafepanini.hu

A high school teacher who got tired of teaching opened this small, bistro-type cafe on the Pest riverfront. It's a dog and child-friendly place. The sandwiches are named after great thinkers, and enjoyed by some of their contemporary descendants. The student waiters are a bit clumsy, giving the term 'slow food' a new meaning.

163 LADÓ CAFÉ

VII. Dohány utca 50.
Erzsébetváros ⑦
+36 70 350 3929
ladocafe.hu

This very traditional cafe takes you back to the 1930s, with jazz concerts every evening at 8. They attract a very different crowd from that of the daily lunch menu, consisting mainly of retired or widowed people who enjoy the classic Hungarian courses. A social safari for the interested traveller.

164 CAFÉ CSIGA

VIII. Vásár utca 2.
Józsefváros ⑥
+36 30 613 2046

'The Snail' is one of the last authentic places on the edge of the square that's changing because of the metro line 4 station. It offers imaginative, affordable lunch menus for the neighbourhood students, artists and young academics. It's a child and dog-friendly place, and a living monument of the transitory times of the 1990s.

165 DUNAPARK

XIII. Pozsonyi út 38.
Újlipótváros ⑨
+36 1 786 1009
dunaparkkavehaz.com

A spacious and classic modern cafe from 1938. It was revived in 2006, but the interior is still original. It takes up two levels and has a great terrace overlooking the park as well as an upstairs space for card players. Its aspirations include a good breakfast, lunch and dinner with piano music. The pastry and ice-cream selection is remarkable.

5 unique cafes with
AN EXTRA TWIST

---

166 PREMIER KULTCAFÉ
VIII. Baross utca 1.
Józsefváros ⑥
+36 30 251 1443
premiercafe.hu

A former cinema, now much more: not only a cultural centre, a cafe, an exhibition hall and an event hall, but also the largest disability-friendly cultural space in Europe today. They provide work for disabled people and the film screenings are subtitled for deaf people. They also serve great sandwiches and drinks.

167 KINO CAFÉ
XIII. Szent István körút 16.
Újlipótváros ⑨
+36 1 781 9453
kinocafe.hu

A small art cinema on Grand Boulevard, with two screening rooms and a pleasant cafe – or a cafe with two cinema rooms, if you like. The lounge is a meeting place for intellectuals, where young poets, with trembling hands, regularly present new work to critics.

168 K:ANTIN

V. Petőfi Sándor
utca 6.
Belváros ①
+36 70 230 7615
katonajozsefszinhaz.hu

This cafe operates in the foyer of Katona
József Theatre (established in 1982), one
of the best theatres in Budapest. In 2012
the entrance part was 'downgraded' under
the influence of the ruin bar aesthetics,
and a bookshop was added. Open from
11 am in the week, only from 4 pm in the
weekend. Card payments only.

169 MAGVETŐ CAFÉ

VII. Dohány utca 13.
Erzsébetváros ⑦
+36 1 205 3395
cafe.magveto.hu

This place is a cross between a cafe, a
bookshop and an event venue and feels
as perfect for 20 as for 80 spectators,
thanks to its smart design. You can buy
the books on display or just enjoy the
nice atmosphere, the good wines and
the super friendly service. Run by a very
funny female blogger.

170 BEOPLAY BP

AT: BÁLNA COMPLEX
IX. Fővám tér 11–12.
Ferencváros ⑥
mylittlemelbourne.hu/
beoplay-bp

Bálna ('the whale' in English) is a
combination of some very old and some
recent buildings. They were meant to be
a Budapest version of Covent Garden. One
of the most elegant shops in the building
is the Bang & Olufsen showroom. The
cafe is attached to that shop. It also has
a terrace, with a great view.

168 K:ANTIN

5 *must-taste*
HUNGARIAN WINES

---

171 **TOKAJ**
WHITE WINE

Out of the 22 wine regions in Hungary, the Tokaj (Toe-Kye) is the only one that's really known outside of the country. Earlier the sweet-tasting Aszú variety was the most popular one – the world's first noble rot wine – but these days the dry varieties (Furmint, Grüner, Riesling) are emerging fast.

172 **VILLÁNY**
RED WINE

These wines come from a warm region in the southwest of Hungary, near the Croatian border, where the soil is volcanic. The red wines produced here are 'lush, structured and elegant' (says the Wine f-Folly Blog). The varieties we recommend to order in a restaurant are Cabernet Franc, Merlot, Kékfrankos and Portugieser. Mind, wine in Hungarian is *bor*.

173 EGER
RED AND WHITE WINE

'Hungarian Burgundy' comes from a region in the northeast of the country. The town of Eger averted a Turkish siege in 1552 and its most famous wine variety, Egri Bikavér ('egg-ree BEE-kah-vaer'), has a story that's related to that infamous siege. By regulation, the blend must be made of at least three kinds of grapes, half of which must be native red grapes.

174 NAGY SOMLÓ

This is the smallest wine region (only 741 acres) in Hungary, north of Lake Balaton. Its unique terroir – a bedrock of black basalt plus ancient lava flows – produces smoky, fiery wines. The top wine is called Juhfark ('you-fark', meaning 'sheep's tail'). It used to be given to women so as to beget a male heir.

175 SPRITZER CRAZE
IN HUNGARY

A spritzer (*fröccs* in Hungarian) is wine diluted with sparkling water and is, of course, very popular in summer. The most frequently ordered varieties are: a big spritzer (2 parts of wine, 1 part of water), a small spritzer (1:1), a long step (1:2), a landlord (4:1), and a caretaker (3:2). They're made with white wine and rosé and served in specialised terraces. People often drink a spritzer standing.

5 wonderful places for
A DRINK IN BUDA

176 CALGARY ANTIK DRINKBÁR
II. Frankel Leó
utca 24.
Víziváros ⑨
+36 20 510 4610

This peculiar institution is a cross between a basement bar and an antique shop. It opened in 1993 and is run by an ex-model and actress, who's always full of stories. Sometimes she refuses to sell particular things, and the opening times are a bit erratic. There is a separate room downstairs for smaller parties. Live piano music.

177 GDANSK BOOKSTORE CAFÉ
XI. Bartók Béla út 46.
Újbuda ⑤
+36 20 988 1873

A tiny cafe and drink bar, with books in Hungarian and Polish. The name is a hint at the nationality of the co-owner, called Marzena. Most tables are occupied by students involved in heated discussions, and academics living next door. Polish beer, vodka and marinated herring are always available.

178 SZATYOR BÁR AND GALLERY
XI. Bartók Béla út 36.
Újbuda ⑤
+36 1 279 0290
szatyorbar.com

This large, colourful and artsy space once used to be a part of the legendary Café Hadik, now next door. The décor and the wall paintings are the work of young artists. Apart from the gallery exhibitions there are concerts, readings, etc.

179 **DÉRYNÉ BISZTRÓ**

I. Krisztina tér 3.
Krisztinaváros ③
+36 1 225 1407
bistroderyne.com

Continuously operating since 1914, this inner Buda grand cafe provides the modern version of the atmosphere of the good old days. They stand for brasserie-style food, great wines and immaculate service, all under the eye of the owners. People come here to see the ruling élite in action, and to be seen. Nevertheless this is also a family-friendly place, especially at brunch time.

180 **BOARD GAME CAFÉ**

XII. Nagyenyed
utca 16.
Hegyvidék ③
+36 70 469 9474
boardgamecafe.hu

A peculiar place in inner Buda: you can play hundreds of board games here, and the attentive staff are always ready to explain the rules of every one of them. There are eight large tables (for up to eight people) and a small one. You have to pay a small entrance fee and then you can stay and play for 3 hours. When you get hungry you can enjoy a panini or a snack.

178 SZATYOR BÁR AND GALLERY

60 PLACES
TO SHOP

---

5 inspiring
BUDAPEST
FASHION DESIGNERS

181 NANUSHKA

V. Bécsi utca 3.
Belváros ①
+36 70 394 1954
nanushka.com

This label was launched in 2005 by Sandra Sandor, who graduated from the London College of Fashion. It's currently available in over 30 countries. All of the clothes are designed in Budapest. The design team aims at building a bridge between intuitive and functional design, resulting in nice clothes that are comfortable to wear.

182 JE SUIS BELLE

V. Ferenciek tere 11.
Belváros ①
+36 70 220 1044
jesuisbelle.hu

One of the few internationally-noted Hungarian fashion brands was launched in 2005. By choosing a non-Hungarian-sounding name they showed their international ambition to make clothes for witty and cool middle-class women who want to stand out. The designers often turn to contemporary fine art and folk art for inspiration, and the lack of unnecessary details is an important aspect of their signature style.

183 LUCKY SHEPHERD

I. Fő utca 63–65.
Víziváros ④
+36 1 610 6891
luckyshepherd.com

The name of this label is the English translation of the last names of the designers: Gabo Szerencsés and Dora Juhász. These ladies emphasise the importance of using textiles of the highest quality and the finest leather. They sell both everyday and formal wear, and they like working with colour. They also design leather accessories like bags, as well as jewellery and notebooks.

184 ÁERON

V. Zrínyi utca 4.
Lipótváros ②
+36 70 931 5765
aeron.hu

Designer Eszter Áron was born in 1981 into a family of tailors. She escorted her mother to international fashion fairs from very early on, and studied fashion and business administration. Her label stands for informal elegance for women, and she's mentioned in every article on Budapest fashion designers. The Áeron showroom is very close to the Four Seasons Hotel, and online orders are shipped worldwide.

185 ROMANI DESIGN FASHION STUDIO

XV. Batthyány utca 31/b.
Rákospalota ④
+36 30 258 9774
romani.hu

This studio was founded by Erika and Heléna Varga, a dress and an accessories designer. They blend Romani traditions and innovation; the outcome is colourful and unique, not necessarily showing the inspiration. Their semi-hidden agenda is to convey messages about acceptance and respect. Also available in the FIAN KONCEPT design shops in the Buda Castle.

5

DESIGNER STORES FOR WOMEN

---

186 NR.3 STORE

V. Szervita tér 3.
Belváros ①
+36 20 383 5984

The name refers to the address, which is a renowned one: this fine art nouveau building was once built for a bank, and is loved especially because of the large golden mosaic on the top. The shop is devoted to three Hungarian designers: 1975 (casual clothes line), AGNESKOVACS (leather bags) and Zwana (modular jewellery).

187 FLATLAB

VIII. Baross utca 3.
(Speakerphone No. 14)
Józsefváros ⑥
+36 30 949 4286

Very near Kálvin tér you'll find this designers' co-op of two fashion designers, Zsófi and Emese, and four graphic designers: Gergő, Dániel, and the two brothers Richárd and Krisztián. This is a combination of a shop and an atelier, where customers can enjoy watching the hectic activities of the hosts.

188 PALOMA ARCADE

V. Kossuth Lajos
utca 14–16. mezzanine
Belváros ①
+36 20 961 9160

Paloma really is a secret, even for most Budapestians. It is a cross between a Covent Garden-like shopping area and an incubator house for emerging Hungarian fashion brands, located in downtown Budapest, and hosts more than 50 up-and-coming talented designers.

189 **EVA'S ROOM**

V. Aulich utca 8.
2nd Fl., door 2, bell 38
Lipótváros ②
evasroom.com

This quiet fashion showroom is on the second floor of an apartment building that also houses Café Liberté (on the ground floor). They represent four brands, and the people behind those brands take turns to keep the shop open.

190 **NON+ SHOWROOM**

VI. Andrássy út 20.
2nd Fl.
Terézváros ⑦
+36 30 253 0193
nonplusz.hu

Upstairs from the chic Café Callas, you'll find the showroom of designer Sarolta Kiss. Her slogan is 'Simple. Pure. Spontaneous' and she also agrees with Mies van der Rohe: 'Less is more'. She prefers a lot of white combined with a little black, and next to seasonal collections she also has about 120 permanent items, as well as a lovely maternity wear collection.

188 PALOMA ARCADE

5 high-end
MEN'S CLOTHING AND SHOE BRANDS

191 VASS SHOES

V. Haris köz 2.
Belváros ①
+36 1 318 2375
vass-shoes.com

László Vass, a luxury shoemaker since 1978, has two shops, near each other. They offer handmade, traditional shoes from the shelves but also 'bespoke shoes' – it takes six weeks to make them especially for you. Mr Vass is also a celebrated art collector, especially since he donated the greater part of his collection to the city of Veszprém.

192 THE SUIT COMPANY
BY APPOINTMENT

V. Galamb utca 4.
Belváros ①
+36 30 636 7732
suitcompany.hu

This is the place to go in Budapest if you urgently need a good suit, made to measure just for you, for whatever reason. You are likely to get an appointment for the same day, or the tailors can come to your office or hotel. They use British (Scabal) or Italian cloth to make you a new perfectly-fitting suit.

193 CROSS & FIELD

XIII. Pozsonyi út 2.
Újlipótváros ⑨
+36 1 239 0097
crossandfield.hu

This is the fourth generation of the family of tailors that created this British sounding brand. They not only represent great suit brands, they also offer great after-sales service, especially when you've ordered a made-to-measure suit. They use the best available materials (Dormeuil, Holland & Sherry, Cerruti, Becker, Gaenslen & Völter).

194 MISTER FÉRFI DIVATHÁZ

V. Irányi utca 1.
Belváros ①
+36 1 267 0598
misterdivathaz.com

They call themselves the Budapest Savile Row, with somewhat lower prices. You can also bring your own suits to have them upgraded. They sell everything you need to complete your outfit: shoes, socks, shirts and accessories. They work with Cerruti, Versace, Luciano Barbera, Valentino, Hilton, and other brands.

195 STAN AHUJA
BY APPOINTMENT

VI. Andrássy út 38.
Terézváros ⑦
+36 1 354 0195
stanahuja.com

If you make an appointment, you can meet Indian-born designer-tailor Stan Ahuja in his shop. He and his team work 60 hours on every suit – it takes six weeks before you can pick it up. They have an even more luxurious service, called In Privato: the tailor comes to you, and consults with you very thoroughly, including several remeasurements, before you give the go-ahead.

The 5 best shops for
ANTIQUES

---

196 PINTÉR ANTIK

V. Falk Miksa
utca 10.
Lipótváros ②
+36 1 311 3030
pinterantik.hu

A tiny entrance hides an underground universe of about 2000 square metres. Paintings, sculptures, pieces of furniture and so on are spread out over about a dozen rooms. A small part of the building is a contemporary gallery, run by Mrs Pintér. Very friendly, knowledgeable staff. In the small courtyard there is a large chimney: it serves the boiler house of the Parliament.

197 ERNST GALÉRIA

V. Irányi utca 27.
Belváros ①
+36 1 266 4016
ernstgaleria.hu

Opposite Café Central you'll find this elegant gallery, run by Austrian-born Ernst Wastl and his beautiful wife, Eleni Korani, originally from Greece – both are respected Hungarians now. They focus on paintings, furniture, ceramics and posters. They have another, smaller shop, near Chain Bridge.

198 MORÓ ANTIK

V. Falk Miksa
utca 13.
Lipótváros ②
+36 1 311 0814
moroantik.hu

Csaba Moró started collecting weapons and oriental artefacts of all kinds as a child, and has continued to do so. He established this gallery in 1993, selling weapons, artefacts and also canes of various types. The gallery is a meeting point for collectors from all over the world.

199 ECSERI FLEA MARKET

XIX. Nagykőrösi
út 156.
Kispest ⑥
+36 20 924 7279

The city flea market was relocated twice after WWII to end up in this location in 1964. It takes half an hour by bus to get there, or 10 minutes by taxi. There are about two dozen shops and a hundred small stalls selling antiques, books, bicycles, chandeliers and old furniture. Today it has become harder to find treasures than it used to be: in communist times the market used to have an aura of freedom – you could buy jeans and Beatles LPs – but those days are gone.

200 BAZÁRUHÁZ ANTIQUE

IX. Mester utca 37.
Ferencváros ⑥
+36 30 234 9009

This corner store, operated by a devoted couple, is like a miniature version of the Ecseri Flea Market. You'll find all kinds of metal bric-a-brac things here, as well as old suitcases, lamps, paper antiques, pens, etc., all in a poetic disorder. Some old people tend to start talking when they bump into you, about what purpose this or that object served. They're looking out for a chance to buy or sell something, and they seem to never give up, just like the owners of this lovely shop.

The 5 most unusual
SPECIALITY SHOPS

---

201 **1001 KEFE**
BRUSHES
VII. Dob utca 3.
Erzsébetváros ⑦
+36 1 322 7344
1001kefe.hu

This family business dates back to 1920. Their selection of (mostly wooden) brushes is immense: from squirrel-hair-based fine artistic instruments to plastic or wire-based industrial tools. They also renovate brushes. The Hungarian saying 'he drinks like a brush maker' means that someone is a heavy drinker.

202 **REFLEXSHOP**
VI. Eötvös utca 39.
Terézváros ⑦
+36 1 269 0941
reflexshop.hu

In a quiet street off Grand Boulevard, you'll find this shop selling all kinds of things for 'active and creative fun'. Think of Rubik's Cubes, boomerangs, yo-yos, sports kites, frisbees, juggling props, powerballs, scooters, poker cards, etc. Also brainteasers are sold here. Obviously, they teach you how to use everything.

203 **NIETSCH-HAJMÁSI**
SHOE ACCESSORIES
VI. Izabella utca 81.
Terézváros ⑦
+36 1 706 6842
cipofuzok.hu

Shoestrings were hard to find during the communist era, at least if you were looking for the right size, length or colour. Here you'll find an amazing variety, all tested by the owners of the shop. Check their website for the shoestring length calculator.

204 BUDAPEST SCHOOL SHOP

XIII. Pozsonyi út 10.
Újlipótváros ⑨
+36 30 438 6368
budapestschool.org

This private school for young children was launched in 2015, by the owners of the Prezi software company. Their shop sells about 400 kinds of books, board games and tech gadgets that train the mind, and help kids learn. There's a large selection of STEM (Science, Technology, Engineering, Math) toys. Popular among tourists as well.

205 GALLWITZ PIPES AND PEARLS

V. Régi posta
utca 7–9.
Belváros ①
+36 30 297 5000
gallwitz-pipa.hu

This little shop sells pipes and pearls, an improbable combination. It has been operating since 1880, but not in the same location: between 1952 and 1962 it was forced to move into an apartment on the second floor. In 1945 they had a chance to promote their business with a movie commercial; it's on their website for you to see. The shop is now run by a great-grandson of the founders.

203 NIETSCH-HAJMÁSI

5 beautiful
FLOWER SHOPS

---

206 RÓZSA VIRÁGÜZLETE

XIII. Pozsonyi
út 11/b.
Újlipótváros ⑨
+36 1 339 8331

An ordinary neighbourhood shop owned by a hardworking somewhat senior lady, Rose. A fitting first name! Fortunately she has assistants to help out when it gets too busy. They have nice, affordable flowers and know their job – they find the right combinations to make a pretty bouquet and wrap it perfectly. Simple, wonderful.

207 SMÚZ CAFÉ

V. Kossuth Lajos
tér 18.
Lipótváros ②
+36 30 954 4200
viragneked.hu

This is an interesting cross between a high-end flower shop and an informal cafe. They serve coffee made on a La Marzocco machine as well as several Japanese teas. The location is priceless: Parliament square, offering a full view of the famous building. They also deliver bouquets in other countries.

208 ARIOSO

VII. Király utca 9.
Erzsébetváros ⑦
+36 1 266 3555
arioso.hu

The flower shop (with a cafe in a different room) takes up the ground floor of an old building with a lovely inner courtyard – in summer you can sit outside. The Swiss owners swear by a 'pure and natural design'. They offer exquisite bouquets and arrangements, mostly for business receptions and celebrity events.

209 PHILANTHIA

V. Váci utca 9.
Belváros ①
+36 70 933 2266

The amazing art nouveau interior of this shop dates back to 1906, and is the reason to visit it. The Greek name means 'love of flowers'. The present owners may share this love, but it seems a bit outshone by the love of profits: the space is overstuffed by nauseating gift items. Still, the wall paintings and the floor tiles are stunning. One is tempted to imagine a different kind of shop here.

210 FITOLAND

VIII. Korányi Sándor utca 2/c.
Józsefváros ⑥
+36 20 432 0050
fitoland.hu/belvaros

This large shop is part of the botanical gardens of the Eötvös University – this is where a substantial part of *The Paul Street Boys* is set, a classic youth novel that's read by all Hungarians. Fitoland is a great place to go for potted plants. Before you go shopping, visit the gardens – they're only one third of the original size, alas.

5
OLD AND RARE BOOKS
shops

---

211 KÖZPONTI ANTIKVÁRIUM

V. Múzeum
körút 13–15.
Belváros ②
+36 1 317 3514
*kozponti
antikvarium.hu*

This large shop still has the somewhat ridiculous-sounding name it got in the communist era: 'Central Antiquarian Bookseller'. There are many sub-sections and a lot of titles in foreign languages, as well as old prints and maps. The best of what they have never finds its way to the shelves: you can buy those treasures at their auctions.

212 TRILLIAN COMICS

VI. Teréz körút 12.
Ground floor No. 2.
(In the courtyard)
Terézváros ⑦
+36 30 739 0085

Since the early 1980s, tiny shops have gradually been taking up the courtyards on Grand Boulevard. This speciality shop has been operating here since 2004, selling original US comics, manga, Hungarian comics, art books, T-shirts, posters, figurines and all kinds of collectors' items. Also a great meeting place for fans of the genre.

213 ATTICUS OLD AND RARE BOOKS

VII. Asbóth utca 19.
Erzsébetváros ⑦
+36 1 351 7361
atticus-antikvarium.hu

This centrally located used books-shop is one for the omnivorous book lover. A unique feature: the owner offers his expertise to build up family libraries for emerging middle-class families. He says that most people should have a family antiquarian, like they should have a family lawyer and a family doctor.

214 KÁRPÁTI AND SON

V. Múzeum körút 29.
Belváros ①
+36 1 318 5857
karpatiesfia.hu

They sell used and rare books as well as old etchings and maps. The latter is evident when you enter the elegant space: several hundred-year-old maps hang from the gallery. Mr Kárpáti has been selling books since 1974 and moved to this location in 2002. Nowadays he holds auctions twice a year.

215 FONT ANTIKVÁRIUM

VI. Andrássy út 56.
Terézváros ⑦
+36 1 332 1646

This shop, run by a drop-out mathematician, is a true delight: places like this prove that the real thing will never be replaced by shopping online. Here you'll find things you never knew you wanted them, or didn't know about up till now. A Köchel list? The first novel of your favourite author? The complete œuvre of Thomas Mann as a graduation gift, for peanuts? It's all here.

The 5 bookshops to go to for
ENGLISH TITLES

---

216 ATLANTISZ KÖNYVSZIGET
V. Anker köz 1–3.
Belváros ②
+36 1 267 6258
atlantiszkiado.hu/ konyvsziget.php

Budapest's highbrow bookshop serves customers with academic interests and offers hundreds of Hungary-related titles in English. It's a super nice shop with a gallery. The little wall space that's not covered with shelves is decorated with old etchings of book worms – the actual insects. The great staff can order anything you might want.

217 BESTSELLERS
V. Október 6. utca 11.
Lipótváros ②
+36 1 312 1295
bestsellers.hu

A misleading name for a serious bookshop. It opened in a former grocery in 1992 and is owned by a jovial Egyptian-born immigrant called Tony Lang. It has a great website to order anything from anywhere in the world. Also an expat meeting place. Open on Sundays.

218 MASSOLIT BOOKS & CAFÉ
VII. Nagy Diófa utca 30.
Erzsébetváros ⑦
+36 1 788 5292

A quiet, idiosyncratic place in the middle of the busy, touristic Jewish district, with a name taken from a Bulgakov novel. There are several little spaces where you can chat or work, and in the foyer you'll find a special table with Hungarian titles in English.

219 RÓZSAVÖLGYI BOOKSHOP

V. Szervita tér 5.
Belváros ①
+36 1 318 3500
rozsavolgyi.hu

One of the oldest bookshops in town, named after a composer and music publisher. It moved to this location in 1911; unfortunately the original interior, was destroyed in a fire in 1963. They're strong in music-related titles, scores and CDs. Upstairs there is a cafe that becomes a small theatre in the evening.

220 KLAUZÁL 13 – BOOKSHOP AND GALLERY

VII. Klauzál tér 13.
Erzsébetváros ⑦
+36 1 413 0731
vincekiado.hu

In 1944 the square where this shop is located used to be the centre of the ghetto; now it's the heart of the ruin pub area. Vince Publishers has long been associated with Taschen, the specialised art books publishers. In the small but nice gallery space you can admire the work of illustrators and other book related projects.

216 ATLANTISZ KÖNYVSZIGET

5 not-to-miss
CONCEPT STORES

———

221 CSENDES CONCEPT STORE

V. Magyar utca 18.
Belváros ①
+36 20 776 2885
csend.es

Related to the cafe and grocer's nearby, this shop sells a wonderful and constantly-changing selection of Hungarian designer stuff – bags, cups, framed prints, cheap jewellery … – for lovers of design and all things cosy. Also on offer: books and unusual cosmetics, packed in metal shoeshine boxes.

222 VIRIVEE

VII. Dob utca 24.
Erzsébetváros ⑦
+36 30 525 6711
virivee.com

This shop sells handmade tights with different patterns – more than 150! You can buy them on their website, but a visit to the real shop is quite an experience. You can talk to the founder/owner, who distorted her own name to create the name of her brand. They ship to over 40 countries.

223 REPERTORY CONCEPT STORE

I. Alagút utca 4.
Krisztinaváros ③
+36 30 639 6559
repertory.hu

This small shop resulted from the cooperation between a clothing and a jewellery designer – Daige and The Mama Kin – who realised that their items match well. It's a cosy shop with coffee and plants, located in a small, emerging shopping street.

224 BP SHOP – WESSELÉNYI

VII. Wesselényi utca 24.
Erzsébetváros ⑦
+36 30 678 4110
bpshop.hu

This streetwear shop launched its own cap brand, using the initials of Budapest: 'BP'. They managed to make their caps the talk of the town, asking trendy young influencers and celebrities to wear them. They also sell all kinds of unusual international brands; their selection will delight streetwear connoisseurs.

225 PRINTA

VII. Rumbach Sebestyén utca 10/a.
Erzsébetváros ⑦
+36 30 292 0329
printa.hu

This large concept and clothes store with a cafe has a distinct ideology: they are all about eco-fashion, silk-screen printing and local, Budapest-made items. This is where you'll find the coolest out-of-the-ordinary bags, T-shirts and framed prints. Also some great stuff for kids, like pillows and other soft items. The shop front was decorated by a contemporary artist.

225 PRINTA

The 5 best shops for
EYEWEAR

---

226 ORANGE OPTIKA SZALON

VI. Király utca 38.
Terézváros ⑦
+36 70 322 2990
orangeoptika.hu

Buying a new pair of glasses is affordable in Budapest, since most retailers offer a free eye examination by a doctor. Take this elegant small shop, for example, and their amazing website. They sell some eccentric, lesser-known international and Hungarian brands. They have a super-friendly staff, who take sides to help you decide which frame suits you best.

227 CONCEPT EYEWEAR

VI. Rózsa utca 71.
Terézváros ⑦
+36 70 638 5757
concepteyewear.hu

A celebrated place to buy handmade frames in the urban jungle of Pest. It takes the craftsmen weeks to make the stylish frames you'll find here, resulting in extra long-lasting quality. They only work with biodegradable materials; they use a lot of wood, often combined with Italian Mazzucchelli acetates.

228 TIPTON EYEWORKS

V. Irányi utca 20.
Belváros ①
+36 1 786 1080
tiptonbudapest.com

The bombastic name fits this place in the centre of Pest perfectly: it's not really a shop, but rather a split-level showroom-and-workshop. They claim to offer the 'largest selection of Vinylize frames in the world'. In the reception area there's a nice framed photo series of people wearing their products. An appointment can be booked in five languages on the website.

229 VISION EXPRESS

XIII. Nyugati tér 5.
Újlipótváros ⑨
+36 1 237 0114
visionexpress.hu

A professional, smooth business, part of a chain, located between Astoria and the National Museum. Some shrewd Budapest people buy frames in trendier shops, and then bring them here to have the glasses inserted at a lower price. By the way, this chain is famous for its speedy service: simpler glasses can be ready in an hour.

230 TREND OPTIKA DI MODA

V. Arany János
utca 12.
Lipótváros ②
+36 1 269 0702
trendoptikadimoda.
trendoptika.hu

This elegant inner-city shop benefits from the proximity of five-star hotels. They offer i4D, VisiOffice technology – they measure your eyes and take a variety of extra factors into consideration, so that they can make the perfect glasses just for you. They have a wide selection of frames, from all over the world.

The 5 best shops for
VINTAGE CLOTHING

231 LUDOVIKA VINTAGE

VII. Rumbach
Sebestyén utca 15.
Erzsébetváros ⑦
ludovika-shop.
tumblr.com

For most people this enchanted street is off the beaten path. You'll find some very special, unique shops here, like this one, run by Krisztina and Dóra. It's a treasure-trove filled with bags and small objects from the good old days, and also shirts, pullovers, jackets, shoes, and even all kinds of wristwatches.

232 LOVEBUG VINTAGE

II. Margit körút 62.
Hegyvidék ③④
+36 30 233 4739
lovebugvintage.com

This 'Hungarian vintage home shop' was started in 2010 by a fashion journalist. It's an inner Buda favourite, and they specialise in T-shirts with funny texts on them and also unicorn-related things. Lovebug also launched the first online vintage shop in Hungary.

233 ANTIFACTORY VINTAGE SHOP

VI. Paulay Ede
utca 43.
Terézváros ⑦
+36 20 255 6228
antifactoryvintage.
tumblr.com

Run by vegan blogger Fanni Stefánkovits, this vintage shop sells 'quirky clothes'. Time seems to have stood still here, and they don't care about trends – one comes here to add a little spice to his or her mainstream attire. The other customers are the main asset of the shop: they're quite a sight.

234 SZPUTNYIK SHOP

VII. Dohány utca 20.
Erzsébetváros ⑦
+36 1 321 3730
szputnyikshop.hu

This is a large, unusual shop selling a combination of vintage clothing and new items. It encourages both men and women to mix the two, and to find themselves a fitting personal style. Their slogan is 'different is beautiful'. The name refers to the title of a Murakami novel (and only indirectly to the Soviet satellite).

235 RETROCK

VI. Anker köz 2–4.
Terézváros ⑦
+36 30 472 3636
retrock.com

This centrally-located shop is the biggest vintage shop in town. It mixes old and new clothes, made by Hungarian or international designers; they import some limited edition series from far-away countries like Korea, Thailand, Peru and Ecuador. You can find great ethno-inspired clothes here. They also sell 'dead stock', i.e. items that have never been worn.

234 SZPUTNYIK SHOP

5 breathtaking

HIGH-END GIFT STORES

---

236 MADISON PERFUMERY

VI. Andrássy út 26.
Terézváros ⑦
+36 1 269 2016
madisonperfumery.hu

This is one of the most sophisticated perfume shops, housed in a former pharmacy from the 1890s; the original furniture was reinstalled in the back room. They sell brands that ordinary mortals have never heard about. They not only sell products, but also give advice and do your make-up.

237 OMOROVICZA

VI. Andrássy út 2.
Terézváros ⑦
+36 1 302 4604
omorovicza.com

The business of this elegant shop has been growing since 2006, offering about 50 expensive creams and ointments, all based on the healing power of Hungarian thermal baths. Mr Omorovicza is a descendent of a Hungarian noble family.

238 ADAM BOSZE MUSIC ANTIQUARIAN

VII. Király utca 77.
(entrance in Csengery utca)
Erzsébetváros ⑦
+36 30 222 7650
musikantiquariat-bosze.eu

Adam Bosze is a cross between a music clown and a serious scholar. His shop is a great place to visit – only by appointment. He mainly sells books, scores and rare prints. An unsigned visiting card of Béla Bartók might not cost you a month's salary. And he might even have a signed one, too.

239 WLADIS GALLERY & STUDIO

V. Falk Miksa utca 13.
Lipótváros ②
+36 1 354 0834
wladisgaleria.hu

This lovely atelier on a corner in the Antique Row of Budapest has two rooms: one is the showroom, the other is the workshop, with old-fashioned instruments and semi-ready silverware. Run by retired design professor Vladimir Péter and his son, this is thé place to go for splendid silver rings and pendants. Their website is a treat in itself.

240 CINQ FILLES

VI. Paulay Ede utca 44.
Terézváros ⑦
+36 30 662 2625
cinqfillesbudapest.com

This is a niche business, the kind you would expect to bump into in London rather than here. They facilitate luxury gift-wrapping by offering boxes of all sizes, colours and materials. You can also have your gifts personalised with ribbons with lettering. They have everything to upgrade the enchanting power of an ordinary gift.

236 MADISON PERFUMERY

35 BUILDINGS TO ADMIRE

5

ARCHITECTS
TO REMEMBER

241 MIKLÓS YBL
1814-1891

The architect that shaped 19th-century Budapest studied in Paris and Munich. His style gradually developed: his older work is an example of Romanticism, his later of Neo-Renaissance. His two Budapest masterpieces are the Opera House (1884) and St Stephen's Cathedral, aka the Basilica (1905). He was also elected to the Upper House.

242 IMRE STEINDL
1839-1902

Steindl was the son of a Pest silversmith, and studied architecture in Budapest and in Vienna. When he was 44 he proposed a design for the Parliament building and got the job. He became the manager of the project, but died six weeks before it was completed. He died partly of disillusionment: younger critics disliked his backward-looking design.

243 **BÉLA LAJTA**
1873-1920

This son of a successful Jewish tailor became the modernist, trend-setting master architect of pre-WWI Budapest. His most important projects include the Institute for the Blind, the Parisiana Cabaret (now New Theatre), the Jewish Grammar School (now Radnóti Gimnázium). If you're interested: admission to the online Béla Lajta Archive is free.

244 **GÁBOR ZOBOKI**
1963-

Zoboki is a classical musician and an architect. He designed the Palace of Arts, with the Bartók Hall inside, and also some major office buildings, for example for Telenor and Nokia. He's also one of the architects of the Corcin Quarter project, and of the National Dance Theatre, which is to be completed in 2019.

245 **SÁNDOR FINTA**
1973-

If not for anything else, he will be remembered as the architect of the two riverbank stations of metro line 4; he said he was inspired by the structure of the human bone. Finta was chief architect of the City of Budapest 2012-2015 project, but was forced out because he was too much dedicated to community-based urban design, which was not appreciated by the mayor.

5 secrets about the
PARLIAMENT BUILDING

V. Kossuth Lajos tér 1-3.
Lipótváros ②
parlament.hu

246 AGE AND SIZE

This amazingly big (265-metre-long) building is one of those buildings in Budapest that try to look much older than they actually are. It was built between 1885 and 1904, when the country was three times as big as it is today, and surpassed its counterpart Vienna (in the dual monarchy of Austria-Hungary) – which explains the size of the building. Inside the Parliament is extremely colourful, and packed with artwork created specifically for the location.

247 BUILDING MATERIAL

Contrary to its appearance this palace – in the style of the Gothic Revival – wasn't built out of stone but of about 40 million bricks. Steel structures carry the weight of the elaborate roofs. It was a state-of-the-art building in its time, with coordinated electric clocks, modern ventilation and many telephone lines.

248 THE DOME

Gothic buildings don't usually have domes; a dome is a style feature of the Baroque. This one is 96 metres high. As is often the case with church domes as well, there is a significant gap between the inner and the outer dome of the Parliament. Had it not been built like that, it would have been either exorbitantly expensive, or unpleasant looking.

249 ILLUMINATED RED STAR

It seems hard to believe, but during the communist period there was an illuminated red star on the top of the dome. It was damaged and repaired several times, for example in 1956, during the revolution, when someone climbed the dome to break it down, but it proved too strong. It was removed in 1990 and now it's on display in the room where Parliament tours end.

250 MAIN ENTRANCE

The main entrance is only opened for heads of states or other state guests, plus once every four years, when newly elected MPs enter the House. There are 29 entrances altogether, but very few of the original ones are used nowadays. Tourists (about half a million per year) use a newly built entrance from the underground Visitor Centre.

The 5 most striking examples of
ART NOUVEAU

---

251 BEDŐ HOUSE

V. Honvéd utca 3.
Lipótváros ②
*magyarszecesszio
haza.hu*

Named after its first owner, Transylvanian copper tycoon Bedő, this 1903 apartment building had some bad days, until it was renovated in 2007. The portals were remade and three apartments were added in the loft space. Nowadays there are a cafe and an art nouveau exhibition area downstairs, and two art galleries upstairs.

252 ROYAL POSTAL SAVINGS BANK

V. Hold utca 4.
Lipótváros ②

The façade of this bank building from 1901 was designed by Ödön Lechner, a great art nouveau master. He used Hungarian folk patterns. The ornaments on the roof are hard to see from the narrow streets, but try to check out the beehives on top of the pilasters and the snakes of the rooftop – they symbolise volatility.

BEDŐ · HÁZ

253 MUSIC ACADEMY

VI. Liszt Ferenc tér 8.
Terézváros ⑦
+36 1 462 4600
zeneakademia.hu

This opulent music palace, filled with paintings and other ornaments, was inaugurated in 1907. In 2013 it reopened after a thorough technical facelift and a restoration, staying true to the building's origins. The courtyards were covered; they now house a nice cafe and a function room. Also air conditioning was installed, but luckily it's very silent.

254 EGGER VILLA

VI. Városligeti
fasor 24.
Terézváros ⑦

This villa was built in the super-chic lane leading up to City Park. It was completed in 1902, as a forerunner of the building style in the street. Look at the wide and asymmetrical windows and balconies. Unfortunately you can't visit the house, so you can't see the incredible wooden stairs inside, luckily you can see photos on your smartphone, standing at the garden gate.

255 SZENT LÁSZLÓ CHURCH

X. Szent László
tér 25.
Kőbánya
+36 1 260 2462
szentlaszlo.net

One of the great buildings that make District X. (it means 'stone quarry') worth visiting is this elegant Catholic church. It was designed by Ödön Lechner and completed in 1899, and it looks like a perfect example of Art Nouveau – at least if you look at the exterior from a distance. Inside it is a hodgepodge of styles – you'll discover Romanesque, Gothic, Baroque and Persian elements.

The 5 most impressive
ARCADES

---

256 FOUR SEASONS HOTEL

V. Széchenyi István tér 5-6.
Lipótváros ②

In 1907 this arcade was built by a London insurance company as an investment. It was neglected during the communist period but renovated and upgraded in 2004. The arcade is the reception area of the Four Seasons hotel now – so just go in, pretend to be looking for a friend, and have a look. Mr Gresham, the founder of the London Exchange, is portrayed in gold at the top of the façade.

257 PARISIAN ARCADE

V. Ferenciek tere
Belváros ①

This building with its Venetian Moorish façade was completed in 1913 and is a symbol of early 20th-century, modern Budapest. It used to be the headquarters of a bank, with apartments upstairs. Decades later a state-owned travel agent operated from here, and now the building is destined to be the five-star Parisian Arcade Hotel (which will open in 2018). The arcade will be open to the public as a cafe.

258 GOZSDU ARCADE

VII. Király utca 13. –
Dob utca 16.
Erzsébetváros ⑦
gozsduudvar.hu

After a renovation in 2008 the Gozsdu Arcade now houses ruin bars, restaurants and escape rooms. It was named after Mr Gozsdu (†1870), a lawyer and a member of Parliament, who left behind a foundation to support Romanian youth to study in Hungary. Decades after his death his money was invested in these seven buildings.

259 RÖSER BAZAAR

Between V. Károly
körút 22. and
Semmelweis utca 19.
Belváros ①
+36 1 429 1300

This quiet courtyard (built in 1884) was once the home of small shops with lower prices than their downtown rivals. Today you still find shops here, but typically more expensive ones, for example high-end boutiques. It's an interesting route to get to the city centre coming from the busy, highway-like Károly körút.

260 VASUDVAR (MILLENNIUM CENTER BUDAPEST)

V. Piarista utca 4.
Belváros ①
+36 1 235 1818
milleniumcenter.hu

In the 19th century this 'iron courtyard' was a busy wholesale and retail hardware shop. Today only the façade survives. Around 2000 it seemed a good idea to recreate the shopping area, with entrances from three sides and a variety of shop spaces on two floors. It didn't really work, as shops and salad bars come and go.

5 *stunning*
CLASSIC MODERN BUILDINGS

261 POST COACH HOUSE
V. Régiposta utca 13.
Belváros ①

This six-storey building from 1938 is a nice example of Bauhaus architecture by Lajos Kozma. Note the terracotta relief above the shop, the red framing of the windows and the 'signature' of the architect. Part of the older building to the left had to be destroyed to create space.

262 'MADÁCH BLOCK'
VII. Károly
körút 13–25.
Erzsébetváros ⑦

This red-brick apartment and office complex was built in 1937-38. It consists of 11 separate blocks and also includes a street. Seventeen older buildings were demolished to make way for it. Is was meant to be the entrance to Elisabeth Avenue – it may be dubbed as 'the entrance to the Most Unfinished Avenue Project in Europe'.

263 DUNAPARK RESTAURANT & COFFEEHOUSE
XIII. Pozsonyi út 38.
Újlipótváros ⑨
+36 1 786 1009
dunaparkkavehaz.com

The neighbourhood north of the Pest side of the Margaret bridge was laid out according to the urban planning rules of the late 1930s, around a sizable park. The most elegant building was completed in 1938, with a cafe downstairs, and fantastic balconies overlooking the river.

264 HEART OF JESUS CHURCH + CAMPANILE

XII. Csaba utca 5.
Hegyvidék ③

When this Catholic church was completed in 1936, it was frowned upon by the higher clergy, and mocked as 'God's garage'. The campanile stands apart from the nave since there is a rivulet underneath, called the 'Devil's Ditch'. The top of the campanile, consisting of cubes, is especially iconic.

265 NAPRAFORGÓ UTCAI KÍSÉRLETI LAKÓTELEP / EXPERIMENTAL VILLA QUARTER

II. Napraforgó
utca 1–22.
Hegyvidék ⑪

This legendary (private) project brought modern Bauhaus architecture in the limelight in 1931–32. A number of small villas were built on equal-sized plots; they all share a number of characteristics, but there are also a few differences. The villas have hardly been altered through the years and remarkably enough the design still feels fresh. Living here still happens with great respect for one's neighbour.

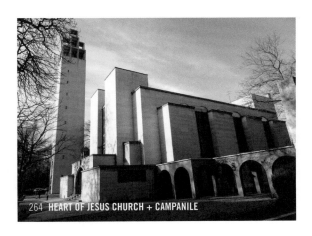

264 HEART OF JESUS CHURCH + CAMPANILE

5 secrets about
BUDAPEST'S BRIDGES

266 CHAIN BRIDGE: THE TOLL YOU HAVE TO PAY

Lipótváros ②

Chain Bridge was built between 1839 and 1849 thanks to the financial support of baron Sina of Vienna. The contract promised him all the toll revenues for 87 (!) years, and it prohibited the construction of other bridges between Buda and Pest. After 21 years already, the investment was returned, including interest. The city then purchased the company – they wanted to build a new bridge.

267 MARGARET BRIDGE, THE CROOKED ONE

Margitsziget ⑨

Margaret Bridge was designed and built by a French company and inaugurated in 1876. At the time, few people understood why it had a break in the middle. The wing leading to Margaret Island wasn't built until 25 years later. At the time of the original opening the island's tip was hundreds of meters away; the gap between the middle of the bridge and the island was later gradually filled up with land.

268 LIBERTY BRIDGE

268 THE MIDDLE SECTION OF LIBERTY BRIDGE

Belváros ①

Many Budapestians consider Liberty Bridge (completed in 1896) the nicest of all bridges in the city. There is an interesting technical detail: the middle 49-metres section of the bridge is not part of the supporting structure. When it was rebuilt after being destroyed during WWII, the celebrated poet Gyula Illyés passed by and immortalised the moment when that middle section was inserted, as the last step.

269 THE MISSING MIRRORS FROM RÁKÓCZI BRIDGE

Ferencváros ⑥

This symbol of the new and free Budapest was completed in 1995 and was known for its peculiarity: it consisted of lamps directed upwards to a series of special mirrors that reflected a dispersed, pleasant kind of light beam on the pavement. Not anymore: maintenance of the mirrors turned out to be too complicated and too expensive.

270 THE OLDER, THE NICER

Belváros ①

Elisabeth Bridge was first completed in 1903. It was damaged severely during WWII but while all the other bridges were rebuilt in their original form after the war, Elisabeth Bridge wasn't: it was widened so it would be able to handle much more, denser car traffic. For this reason a large part of the Old Town of Pest had to be demolished.

5 stunning
21ST-CENTURY
BUILDINGS

271 HAPIMAG RESORT BUDAPEST

I. Fortuna utca 18.
Várnegyed ④
+36 1 487 7400
hapimag.com

This corner in the Castle District used to house nothing more than some medieval ruins. The district refused ideas about a new destination for decades, until the present design was proposed by Péter Reimholz and completed in 2000 (it was the architect's last project). It's a perfect blend of old and new elements, combining stone, wood, metal and glass. It will never grow old.

272 ING BUILDING

VI. Dózsa György út 48.
Terézváros ⑦

The Dutch banking company ING is known for commissioning iconic buildings all over the world. This large office block overlooking City Park is a love or hate affair for locals. It reflects how uncertain and instable the 21st century feels – it looks as if it's held together by the chromium ribbon around it. It was designed by the Rotterdam and Budapest based architect Erick van Eggeraat and was completed in 2004.

273 BÁLNA BUDAPEST

IX. Fővám tér 11–12.
Ferencváros ⑥
balnabudapest.hu

The city wanted to make use of the old storage spaces from 1881 – that's how the idea to build this centre was born. Kas Oosterhuis won the design competition. Although the project was marred with scandals, and failed to meet expectations, it is a symbol of new Budapest.

274 GRAPHISOFT PARK

III. Záhony utca 7.
Óbuda ⑩
+36 1 815 3400

On the site of a closed-down gas factory, on a large riverbank lot, you'll find this state-of-the-art science and office park, consisting of more than a dozen buildings. Two universities operate here: a new one, which was launched by Graphisoft Park owner Gábor Bojár, and an existing one, which moved into the old office buildings. The lush green setting, with lots of water, is a big plus.

275 CEU EXTENSION

V. Nádor utca 15
Lipótváros ②
+36 1 327 3000
ceu.edu

The Central European University was established in the early 1990s by the Hungarian billionaire and philanthropist George Soros, and has expanded substantially since then, in two phases. The most recent buildings were designed by O'Tuomey + Donnell, who earned praise for respecting the (Dublin) architectural heritage on the site and adding natural light to unexpected spaces. The cafe is open to the public. Try to get a pass to the library.

MONTEVERDI

55 PLACES TO DISCOVER BUDAPEST

The 5 best
VIEWS OF BUDAPEST

---

276 CITADELLA FORTRESS
XI. Gellérthegy
Újbuda ⑤

This widely known and sombre fortress was built in 1851 by the Habsburgs to keep Buda and Pest under control, but it was never really used – 16 years later the dual monarchy was established. It was occupied by the Austrians until 1897, when the city took over the site. Some parts of its walls were destroyed by the city authorities, but most of the structure still stands.

277 IN FRONT OF THE STATUE OF PRINCE EUGENE OF SAVOY
I. Budavári Palota
Várnegyed ④

The medieval Buda Castle was destroyed in 1686 when the Habsburgs liberated Buda. A new palace was built piecemeal in the following decades, and the statue of the Austrian general who cleared Hungary of the Turks was placed there in 1900. The view is superb: all Pest is at our feet.

278 BATTHYÁNY TÉR

I. Batthyány tér
Víziváros ④

This pretty square, with some early 18th-century houses, two churches and two statues, became more important when the metro station opened in 1972. The best place to enjoy the view is the riverfront, right opposite the Parliament building. This is also a perfect place to get a good look at the bridges, Gellért Hill and the cathedral dome.

279 THE MIDDLE OF MARGARET BRIDGE

Between Buda
and Pest, at the tip
of the island ⑨

For a mighty view look southwards, away from Margaret Island – you'll be looking at a sort of 'third bank' of the Danube. You'll see Gellért Hill and three or four bridges, and then as far as the new Millennium Quarter, including the controversial, schmaltzy National Theatre. The cross on the stone crown right in front of you regularly gets stolen by vandals.

280 PANORAMA DECK OF VIGADÓ CONCERT HALL

V. Vigadó tér 2.
Belváros ①
+36 20 429 4124
vigado.hu

Vigadó is a word thought up especially to name this building: 'a place to be merry'. It was built by architect Frigyes Feszl in 1865, but after it was seriously damaged during the war, it remained unused for decades. During the latest renovation a panorama deck was added, oriented towards Buda. It's a nice place for a rest after a visit of the building.

5 relics from
ROMAN TIMES

281 CONTRA AQUINCUM
V. Március tér 15.
Belváros ①

Though the Pest side of the city never belonged to the Roman Empire, this fortress was built here anyway. It was huge – some parts of the ruin were unearthed and then covered by glass to give visitors an idea. Also interesting is the drawing of the river line carved into the pavement, showing the fortresses alongside.

282 AQUINCUM MUSEUM
III. Szentendrei
út 135.
Óbuda ⑩

Under the Roman rule, Hungary belonged to the 'Pannonia Inferior' province. The capital was called Aquincum: nowadays this is District III. In the 1890s the civilian parts of the former Roman city were unearthed, and a small museum was built on the site.

283 THE AMPHITHEATRE
III. Nagyszombat
utca
Óbuda ⑩

In Aquincum there were two amphi-theatres: one for the soldiers and one for the civilians; this is the first one. It's hard to believe, but this fighting arena (90×60 metres) is bigger than that of the colosseum in Rome. It was built in 145 AD, under emperor Antonius Pius.

284 THERMAE MAIORES

III. Flórián tér 3–5.
Óbuda ⑩

The bulk of this vast bathing house was unearthed accidentally in the early 1980s, when workmen were drilling holes for columns to support the fly-over. Overnight the engineers had to decide what to do. They chose to save the finds, to make the news public, and not to meet their deadline. The floor plan of the building is amazingly complex.

285 HADRIAN'S PALACE

III. Óbudai sziget
Óbuda ⑩

The largest and most opulent Roman find was discovered and documented in the 1940s and 1950s, but it was covered up with earth again, to be safeguarded for later generations. The site is located in the former docklands, now this is where you'll find several youth clubs. Scientists think the palace might have been built between 104 and 106 AD by the governor of Pannonia, who later became the Emperor Hadrianus.

5 places to
UNDERSTAND
BUDAPEST

---

286 METRO ESCALATOR IN DEÁK FÉRENC TER

V. Deák Ferenc tér
Belváros ①

In Deák tér three underground lines meet, making it a perfect place for people-watching. It's worthwhile going up and down the escalators of Metro 2 a couple of times, to get a sample of Budapest people from all walks of life. In a half-modernised society, most Budapest people don't hide emotions.

287 WESTEND CITY CENTER (BEFORE CHRISTMAS)

VI. Váci út 3.
Terézváros ⑦

This is the most central shopping centre, with over 400 shops. It offers some interesting views, especially from the roof garden. You can look down from upstairs, and feel like Gulliver, watching the Lilliputians down below 'trampling' each other.

288 QUEUEING FOR CHAIN BRIDGE IN A CAR, PEST SIDE

V. Széchenyi Lánchíd
Lipótváros ②

Chain Bridge has only one lane in each direction, meaning that the three lanes leading up to it have to merge. Everyone knows which lane leads to the bridge directly, but hundreds of drivers seem to realise only at the last moment that they want to go on the bridge, thus punishing the honest ones.

289 SZÉLL KÁLMÁN TÉR TRAFFIC JUNCTION

II. Széll Kálmán tér
Víziváros ④ /
Hegyvidék ⑰

For decades this was one of the noisiest, dirtiest places in the city, with a 'market' where employers came to hire unskilled labourers for the day. In 2015 the site was renewed and it became a welcoming and much more nice-looking meeting point. The original and iconic clock was moved to a city museum, and a new concrete clock tower was placed on the same spot, with an image of the old one on its side.

290 SZÉCHENYI BATHS OUTDOOR POOL

XIV. Állatkerti
körút 9–11.
Zugló ⑧
+36 1 363 3210
szechenyispabaths.com

Széchenyi is the biggest public bath and its public is an interesting mix of people with many different social backgrounds and nationalities: you'll see local city dwellers here, but also British stag party participants, Budapest-based diplomats, senior citizens, affluent gypsy business people and also many kids. The open-air bath is also popular in winter.

289 SZÉLL KÁLMÁN TÉR

5 *charming*
SMALL SQUARES
and GARDENS

---

291 MÁRIA TÉR
I. Mária tér
Víziváros ④

A little triangular square in inner Buda, with a baroque Pest-memorial from 1724 in the centre. There is also a themed playground here, which is all about Rumini, a little boy mouse who finds his vocation as a seaman on a seagoing ship. Also worth a visit is the tiny workshop of the Fortepan Photo Archive.

292 CSARNOK TÉR
IX. Csarnok tér
Ferencváros ⑥

Behind the Parisian-like central food market hall there is this nice square with a secondhand shop, a quality wine shop and a large cafe. Let's hope the large newly constructed hotel will not disrupt the scale of life here. Anyway, its arrival is good news for the classical and jazz music venue BMC just around the corner.

293 KAMERMAYER KÁROLY TÉR
V. Kamermayer Károly tér
Belváros ①

A nice, small square, tucked away in the Inner City, with a statue of the first mayor of unified Budapest, who gave the square its name. The centre of life here is Café Gerlóczy, on the ground floor of a small boutique hotel.

294 HORVÁTH MIHÁLY TÉR

VIII. Horváth
Mihály tér
Józsefváros ⑥

This square was named after the bishop and historian whose statue is near the church. His statue used to be on a far more central location in town, but the communists did not like him so much so they moved him to this spot. But what this square is really known for is the Fazekas grammar school and its specialised math classes: generations of great mathematicians graduated here.

295 KÁROLYI KERT

V. Károlyi kert
Belváros ①

This large garden used to be closed; it was the private property of the owners of the adjacent aristocratic palace, which now houses the Museum of Literature. Today the romantic garden is open to the public and despite its central location, it is a peaceful place for a rest. You can find good coffee at the cafe just outside the fence, and some interesting galleries in the near.

295 KÁROLYI KERT

5 things to know about the
OPERA HOUSE

VI. Andrássy út 22.
Terézváros ⑦
+36 1 814 7100
opera.hu

296 THE FAÇADE

The Budapest Opera building was completed by 1884. The budget didn't allow for the building to be covered with limestone all around, so most of the sides and the back part were finished with plaster. Left and right of the entrance there are the two greatest composers of Hungary, Liszt and Erkel, although the latter is hardly known abroad.

297 TWO SETS OF STATUES OF COMPOSERS ON THE OPERA

Originally there were 16 statues of composers but they were removed in the late 1930s, because they were in such bad shape. In the 1960s new statues were commissioned, and apart from six obvious choices, ten new names appeared: Donizetti, Verdi, Bizet and three Russian composers, plus Smetana and Moniuszko – to flatter fellow communist countries.

298 THE STORY OF THE CANDLE MONEY

Not long after the opening of the Opera House in 1884, in a time when musicians played by candlelight so as to be able to read their scores, the leader of the musicians' union approached the director and asked for 'candle money' for the musicians, and he got what he wanted. Some years later electricity was installed, but thanks to their influential trade union musicians kept receiving their candle money until 1929.

299 INTENDANT PODMANICZKY'S CANDY

Baron Frigyes Podmaniczky was the first intendant of the Opera and he was known for his peculiar way of praising and scolding soloists. After premieres, he took all the singers apart one by one: he gave three sweets to the singers who had given an outstanding performance, two to the ones with bearable performances, and one sweet to the singers whose performance had been inferior.

300 THE ROYAL BOX

When King Francis Joseph and Queen Elisabeth attended the opening night of the Opera, they ascended the Royal Staircase. Today tradition still dictates that the Royal Box is only opened for heads of states or prime ministers, Hungarian or foreign. But all the boxes are elegant, and you can you order champagne over there.

5

UNDERGROUND SECRETS

301 'BIRTH OF THE CITY' STATUE

Kálvin tér
Underground
Passage
Belváros ①

In the early 1980s the city of Budapest commissioned a statue, to be titled *Birth of the City*. It was this design by Gyula Illés that was chosen. When you take a closer look, you'll see that it depicts a giant female sex organ. Everybody expected prudish communist censors to intervene, but they didn't, and unveiled the mural in 1983.

302 KÁNYÁDI BENCH

M3 Arany János
utca station
Lipótváros ②

The poem *Vanity* by the Transylvanian poet Sándor Kányádi is a playful homage to a bench in the metro station that was named after 19th-century poet János Arany: 'I dare not wish more, just a bench at the metro station Arany János Budapest.' His wish came true in 2003.

303 THEIRESIAS STATUE

M2 Kossuth Lajos tér
station, downstairs
Lipótváros ②

When this statue was unveiled, the sitting man still had a stick, but it didn't take long before that stick was stolen. It was replaced once, but not a second time. The title, carved in the dark granite surface, says *Tiresias*, the name of the blind fortuneteller in the *Iliad*. An artwork hardly fit for a public space.

304 PORTUGUESE WALL TILES

**M3 Deák Ferenc
tér station
Belváros** ①

Few Budapestians know the story behind
these colourful tiles: they form a work of
art by João Vieira. The complicated piece
shows Portuguese poems in Hungarian
and vice versa. If you're told this, you can
make up some names if you stare at it
intensively, but not much more. The work
of art was an official gift to Budapest from
its sister city Lisbon in 1996.

305 'MOTHER AND CHILD' STATUE

**M2 Kossuth Lajos
tér – foyer
Lipótváros** ②

There was no specific reason to erect
this statue in 1972, shortly after the
inauguration of this metro station, other
than that it was trendy in a modernist
way. The maker, József Somogyi, was the
dean of the art academy and a member of
the communist 'parliament'; so not really
a man in need of more commissions.
The statue seems to have become more
interesting some decades later.

304 PORTUGUESE WALL TILES

5 interesting
CEMETERIES

306 FIUMEI ROAD CEMETERY
VIII. Fiumei út 16–18.
Józsefváros ⑥
+36 70 400 8632
fiumeiutisirkert.nori.gov.hu

The nicest one. This cemetery is often called the Budapest Père Lachaise. It was opened in 1849 and is the final resting place of several dozens of artists and politicians, most of them with fitting edifices. Since 2016 it is no longer owned by the city of Budapest but by the state. There is a small museum inside the gates, as well as a new visitors centre.

307 SALGÓTARJÁNI UTCA JEWISH CEMETERY
VIII. Salgótarjáni utca 6.
Józsefváros ⑥
+36 1 896 3889
zsidotemeto.nori.gov.hu

The most exotic one. This place looks like an enchanted, neglected garden, where nature has overgrown hundreds of lavish, large tombstones. These were erected by and for the pre-WWI Jewish élite, who made Hungary great. It is a rare but fine amalgam of styles: Art Nouveau, Modernism and Hungarian folk motifs. A number of tombstones were designed by Béla Lajta, a genius architect who died at a young age.

308 FARKASRÉTI CEMETERY

XII. Némethvölgyi
út 99.
Hegyvidék ⑪
+36 1 248 3520

Buda's biggest. A rare phenomenon: a cemetery with a panoramic view. This is a municipally-maintained place with special sections for artists of all kinds, and for deceased members of the Academy of Sciences. The funeral home was designed by organic architect Imre Makovecz; inside it looks like a whale skeleton.

309 THE COURTYARD OF GREAT SYNAGOGUE

VII. Dohány utca 2.
Erzsébetváros ⑦
+36 1 343 0420
dohany-zsinagoga.hu

The most centrally located. Jewish cemeteries tend to be away from synagogues; this exception is in consequence of the horrible events at the Ghetto in 1944-45. Of the more than 70.000 inhabitants here, over 10.000 died. Most of them were buried according to tradition, but 2281 people ended up in 24 common tombs.

310 PART OF NEW PUBLIC CEMETERY

X. Kozma utca 8–10.
Kőbánya
+36 1 433 7356

The most politically smitten. This cemetery opened in 1886 and was extended five times in the course of the years. As it turned out in the late 1980s, the furthest, unkempt parcel, no. 301, was used to bury the people who were executed after the 1956 revolution, including Prime Minister Imre Nagy. There's a series of memorials there now – some beautiful, some kitschy ones.

The 5
FOUNDING FATHERS
of Budapest

---

311 ARCHDUKE JOSEPH, THE PALATINE
1776-1847

As the son of one emperor, and the brother of another, he was sent to Hungary to serve Habsburg interests. He did so with a feel for progress; he initiated many Pest-related good causes from the National Museum to creating City Park. He served for 51 years, and his statue was the first public statue of a man to be erected in Pest.

312 COUNT GYULA ANDRÁSSY
1823-1890

This hero of the Hungarian Revolution of 1848–49 was called back from exile to be the first Prime Minister of semi-independent Hungary in 1867. He was an Anglomaniac, and he established the Council of Public Works to carry out large city projects. His equestrian statue stands south of the Parliament building, which he helped to build.

313 FRIGYES PODMANICZKY, THE 'CHECKED BARON'

1824-1907

Budapest wouldn't be the modern metropolis it is if not for this larger-than-life figure. For many years he was the acting chairman of the Council of Public Works and thus the initiator of Grand Boulevard, Andrássy út, three bridges and other architectural projects. He got his nickname because of his eccentric dress code.

314 MAYOR ISTVÁN BÁRCZY

1866-1943

A great social reformer and builder of important schools. During his tenure of office the gas, electricity and tram companies came into municipal owner-ship. He was also sensitive to housing problems. He is remembered as a workaholic, and as a crossing between an innovator and an administrator. One of the streets around City Hall bears his name.

315 MIHÁLY RÁDAY, TELEVISON ANCHORMAN

1942-

He was the anchorman of a TV programme on preserving architectural heritage that was on air between 1979 and 2011. He single-handedly managed to change public opinion on the value of buildings from the past. After 1990, he was a member of the free parliament and also a city councillor, but he wasn't fit for party politics; he rather was a lonely crusader, a nay-sayer.

5 important
TRENDSETTERS
IN THE ARTS

316 **PÉTER EÖTVÖS**
1944-

This world-renowned classical composer conducts his own (and very successful) operas and has a foundation that focusses on creating chances for young musicians. He has lived and worked in cities all over the world, but is spending more and more time in Budapest, striving to put the city on the map of the international cultural scene, using his connections.

317 **IVAN FISCHER**
1951-

Conductor Ivan Fischer studied in Vienna and lived in Holland, and was already successful when he established the Budapest Festival Orchestra in 1982 – today this is one of the top ten ensembles of the world. He believes in meticulously rehearsing rather than in last-minute miracles. He thinks of all members of the orchestra as soloists. He is also a crusader for programmes for children.

318 ILDIKÓ ENYEDI
1955-

The fragile-looking *petite* female film director has only a few films to her name, but all of them are internationally acclaimed. Her 2017 film, *On Body and Soul*, was shot 18 years after the previous one, and won the main prize of the Berlinale Festival. She is a marked critic of injustice, in Hungary and elsewhere, protesting in her low-key, but persistent way.

319 LÁSZLÓ GŐZ
1954-

Originally a trombone player and music publisher, musician and cultural manager László Gőz also tried his hand at organising large concerts. He invested his money in the establishment of the Budapest Music Center; it took about ten years and some extra public funding in the end to realise it. It's a venue for classical and jazz concerts with recording spaces and a library, and even a little hotel.

320 BÉLA PINTÉR
1970-

A natural talent: Béla Pintér writes the plays for his company, he directs all the productions, and he acts in all of them as well. His famous quip: "The government that was in charge before 2010 gave me money, the present one gives me subjects to write plays on." He's internationally successful – for example, he was invited by Barishnikoff Arts Center to play in New York.

5 *perfect*
PARKS AND GARDENS FOR JOGGERS

---

321 MARGARET ISLAND / MARGITSZIGET

Between Buda and Pest, between Margaret and Árpád bridges ⑨

Named after a medieval princess this is a kind of Central Park of Budapest, with a great jogging track, a swimming pool and an all-year-round beach called Palatinus. At the northern tip there are two hotels. Until 1919 Margaret Island was privately-owned and people had to pay an entrance fee. You can get to the park by bus or water bus.

322 CITY PARK / VÁROSLIGET

Zugló ⑧

Two hundred years ago this was the first planned public park in the world, and it has grown into more than just a green oasis: it is also home to institutions of culture, entertainment and recreation like the Museum of Fine Arts. To make the park 21st-century proof it will get a complete facelift: the institutions will be renovated and the park's green area will be rehabilitated and enlarged. The – controversial – project will be completed by 2020.

323 KOPASZI-GÁT
Újbuda ⑤

South of the Lágymányos Bridge, on the Buda side, you'll find this nice park, with a large pond in the middle of it. It was the first step of a successful city gentrification project on a former industrial site. There are nice restaurants and cafes, a playground, a rekortan running track and even an award-winning building that houses the water police station.

324 NÉPLIGET
Kőbánya

The biggest public park in Budapest is also the most neglected and undervalued one. For many decades it was used as a motorcycle race site and a practice ground for wannabe drivers, and it has never really recovered from that period. However, 'Walking Solar System' is a nice garden project: it's about 650 metres long and it represents the solar system on a 1: 10 billion scale.

325 VÉRHALOM TÉR
Hegyvidék ⑪

A square with a bus terminus, on the top of Rose Hill, a traditionally chic middle-class area. The park is never really crowded – young mothers from the neighbourhood like to come here when they want to get out of the house, or students who need a little distraction. There's a 415-metre-long rekortan running track.

5 great
WALKING TOURS

326 BEYOND BUDAPEST

+36 20 332 5489
beyondbudapest.hu

They were the first company to offer socio-cultural tours, in the at the time not very trendy District VIII. – or as a writer once put it, in the 'thousand times blessed' Joseph Town. Since then they also offer tours elsewhere, e.g. the Gas Works tour, the enchanted Jewish Cemetery tour or the Inner City Secrets tour.

327 HOSSZÚLÉPÉS. JÁRUNK?

V. Zoltán utca 18.
Lipótváros ②
+36 70 313 6137
hosszulepes.org

With a staff of ten, this is the best-known organisation on the urban-walk-market. They are resourceful and flexible, and they are perfect for small groups or companies. On the 144th birthday of the city they attached a balloon to well over a hundred statues, and placed a paper crown on the bronze and stone heads.

328 ABSOLUT WALKING TOURS

VI. Lázár utca 16.
Terézváros ⑦
+36 1 269 3843
absolutetours.com

This international company has been operating in Budapest since 1999. They offer many different walks, with themes like Communism, WWII, Jewish life in Budapest or 1956. They also organise tours to experience things like beer and wine tastings, a pub-crawl, and a night stroll.

329 SÉTAMŰHELY

V. Sas utca 14.
Lipótváros ②
+36 70 408 6888
setamuhely.hu

This company probably organises the most specialised tours. They call themselves a 'community forming, memory processing' company, and on their walks you'll learn about, for example, Bauhaus architecture, the world of Imre Kertész, a nun who saved Jewish lives during the war, and the Turks in Buda Castle.

330 IMAGINE BUDAPEST

V. Királyi Pál utca 18.
Belváros ①
+36 20 454 1916
imaginebudapest.hu

This family-based venture offers thematic sightseeing tours with expat guides. There are more general alternative tours and some very specific ones on themes like 'Crime and History in Buda Castle' or 'Message Walls' during which you'll decipher information left behind by generations long gone.

SZTEHLO STATUE

50 PLACES
TO INDULGE IN
CULTURE

5 not-so-obvious but inspiring
CULTURAL CENTRES

---

331 BARTÓK MEMORIAL HOUSE

II. Csalán út 29.
Hegyvidék ⑪
+36 1 394 2100
bartokmuseum.hu

Béla Bartók (1881-1945), the greatest Hungarian composer of all times, actually lived in this rented villa from 1932 to 1940, before he emigrated to the US. These days the villa houses an intimate concert hall (upstairs) and a museum, in the three rooms where the composer used to work. All the furniture is original; it was donated by one of Bartók's sons.

332 MAI MANÓ HOUSE

VI. Nagymező
utca 20.
Terézváros ⑦
+36 1 473 2666
maimano.hu

This amazing eight-storey building, which was completed in 1894, is devoted entirely to photography. It was built and used by the phenomenally successful Manó Mai (1854-1917), a commercial portrait photographer. Since 1999 it houses a professional fine art photo gallery, exhibition spaces and a bookshop. Don't miss the daylight studio on the second floor, which was restored in its original 19th-century splendour and boasts some wonderful frescoes that served as the background on Manó Mai's photographs.

333 CIRKO-GEJZIR ART CINEMA

V. Balassi Bálint
utca 15–17.
Lipótváros ②
+36 1 269 1915
cirkofilm.hu

A three-room cinema in a riverfront basement, with a tiny entrance and a very stylish foyer, where even the clock is a moving image on a flat screen. Films are always in the original language, with subtitles. Maintained by a foundation. Part of the Europa Cinemas network, subsidised by the European Union.

334 METROPOLITAN ERVIN SZABÓ LIBRARY

VIII. Szabó Ervin
tér 1.
Józsefváros ⑥
+36 1 411 5000

Budapest has a great public library network. Since 1931 its central building is in a neo-baroque aristocratic palace from the late 1880s. In 2000 two new wings were added. There are about a dozen different reading rooms, the glitziest of which is the art history room. The cafe is in the former stables. Coffee still should be better.

335 BMC – BUDAPEST MUSIC CENTER

IX. Mátyás utca 8.
Ferencváros ⑥
+36 1 216 7894
bmc.hu

Opened in 2013, this place is a mecca for music lovers. It was built and is now directed by the jazz trombone player-turned-visionary-cultural-manager László Gőz. It houses half a dozen institutions: a concert hall, a jazz club, a music library, a recording studio, the Peter Eötvös Foundation, and even a small hotel for workshop participants. It's a private institution, sustained with some public funding.

The 5 best
ART GALLERIES

336 ACB GALLERY
VI. Király utca 76.
Terézváros ⑦
+36 1 413 7608
acbgaleria.hu

This contemporary art gallery with its Spartan name (which is easy to misspell) opened in 2003 and has three small exhibition areas. The gallery is for up-and-coming and mid-career neo-avant-garde artists. They organise events for a close circle of collectors, and try hard to link contemporary art to an audience.

337 VINTAGE PHOTO GALLERY
V. Magyar utca 26.
Belváros ①
+36 1 337 0584
vintage.hu

Attila Pőcze has put photography on the Budapest gallery map. He sells modern (i.e. 20th-century) and contemporary prints by Hungarian artists – all of them are duly itemised on the website. He never misses Paris Photo nor some other art fairs. His gallery overlooks a lovely secret green spot downtown.

338 KNOLL GALLERY
VI. Liszt Ferenc tér 10.
Terézváros ⑦
+36 1 267 3842
budapest.knollgalerie.at

Hans Knoll has sister galleries in Vienna and Budapest. He has been representing artists in Budapest for over 20 years. His Budapest gallery is housed in a first-floor apartment in a busy square with many cafes, and is very influential in the art scene.

339 VÁRFOK GALLERY
I. Várfok utca 11.
Várnegyed ④
+36 1 489 3920
varfok-galeria.hu

Gallerist Károly Szalóky opened his gallery in 1990, when communism ended and Hungary was free again. Thanks to him Várfok utca gradually became known as a gallery street. His gallery consists of two spaces, plus 19 triangular-shaped glass boards around 19 trees along the sloping street, showcasing reproductions printed on foil.

340 DEÁK ERIKA GALLERY
VI. Mozsár utca 1.
Terézváros ⑦
+36 1 201 3740
deakgaleria.hu

Around the corner of a busy neighbourhood nicknamed 'The Broadway of Pest', Erika Deák represents several artists – mostly painters, Hungarian as well as foreign. She works from this space but also regularly attends major art fairs abroad. Attila Szűcs is the biggest name on her list: he's a major figure in the Budapest arts scene.

337 VINTAGE PHOTO GALLERY

5 great
CINEMAS
with an interesting past

---

341 URÁNIA
VIII. Rákóczi út 21.
Józsefváros ⑥
+36 1 486 3400
urania-nf.hu

Originally built for a 'science slide show' in 1894 in the Moorish Revival style, this large cinema was completely renovated in 2002. It's maintained by the government, and is a great place to attend festivals and film premieres, but also English and American theatre and opera broadcasts. There are two small rooms downstairs as well.

342 PUSKIN
V. Kossuth Lajos
utca 18.
Belváros ①
+36 1 224 5650
puskinmozi.hu

Opened in 1926 as Forum, this cinema is one of the best art kinos in town, with three screening rooms. In 1929 it was the first cinema to show a talking picture in Hungary. It was renamed Puskin in 1948, after the communist coup d'état. Unlike other cinemas, it didn't get back its old name in 1990.

343 KINO CAFÉ
XIII. Szent István
krt. 16
Újlipótváros ⑨
+36 1 781 9453
kinocafemozi.hu

A lovely two-room art cinema on Grand Boulevard, near Margaret Bridge. Though the name means 'cinema' in Russian, the cinema was actually named after a pop band. Occasionally small festivals are organised here, in honour of architectural films. There's a great cafe in the foyer.

344 MŰVÉSZ

VI. Teréz körút 30.
Terézváros ⑦
+36 1 224 5650
muveszmozi.hu

During the interwar period this was a 'cinema with a bell': they rang a bell as a sign for couples to stop cuddling. Nowadays it's a six-room art kino, on Grand Boulevard, with performances from 1 pm onwards, and earlier in the weekend. It also offers the best art video rental service in town with well over 10.000 DVDs and great personal advice.

345 CORVIN

VIII. Corvin köz 1.
Józsefváros ⑥
+36 1 224 5650
corvinmozi.hu

Originally built in 1924, this was Budapest's largest cinema for many years. It played an important role in the 1956 revolution, a fact that's commemorated with a statue and with some plaques with unreliable facts. In 1996 it was converted into a multiplex cinema. It's still owned by the city.

341 URÁNIA

The 5 smallest
MUST-VISIT MUSEUMS

---

346 HOUSE OF TERROR
VI. Andrássy út 60.
Terézváros ⑦
+36 1 374 2600
terrorhaza.hu

House of Terror provides 'infotainment': it's a playful, ironic museum on totalitarian regimes in Hungary, housed in an authentic building – it was the headquarters of the Hungarian fascist party during WWII and later on that of the communist secret police. It's full of black humour. The English audioguide is a must.

347 STAMP MUSEUM
VII. Hársfa utca 47.
Erzsébetváros ⑦
+36 1 342 3757
belyegmuzeum.hu

This modernist post office building from 1937 has always included this museum space, with hundreds of vertical wooden trays filled with stamps stored under glass. Stamps, together with physical letters, are an endangered species in Hungary – that's why this pretty museum is so nice, especially for anyone who has ever collected stamps.

348 MEMENTO PARK – COMMUNIST STATUE THEME PARK

XXII. Corner of Balatoni út and Szabadkai út
Budatétény ⑤
+36 1 424 7500
mementopark.hu

When communism was abolished in Budapest the city council was in doubt: what to do with the statues honouring the important figures of the period? Instead of destroying them (they are of varying quality), this park was established to house all those sculptures of Marx, Lenin and many minor working class heroes. It is a carefully planned park, and it's worth walking the path. A 20-minute taxi drive from the town centre.

349 LISZT MÚZEUM

VI. Vörösmarty utca 35.
Terézváros ⑦
+36 1 322 9804
lisztmuseum.hu

Franz Liszt, the pianist and Romantic-era composer, actually lived here, in the old Music Academy – the museum is his former apartment. Outside, beside the door, you can still see the brass plaque that said when he was at home (Tue-Thu-Sat from 3 to 4 pm) in case you wanted to meet him. Plus authentic furniture, instruments, scores, paintings and photos.

350 RÓTH MIKSA EMLÉKHÁZ

VII. Nefelejcs utca 26.
Erzsébetváros ⑦
+36 1 341 6789
rothmuzeum.hu

Miksa Róth was a prolific stained glass maker – he was a contractor of the parliament and of many banks – and also the producer of colourful mosaics. This building was his home and workshop, and now gives an overview of his career. Born Jewish, he was forced to close his business in 1939. He died here in his bed in 1944.

5 *influential*
CONTEMPORARY ARTISTS

---

351 AKOS BIRKAS
1941-

A painter who's well-known outside Hungary. Even though he draws like Dürer, he made abstract paintings for about two decades. In the mid 2000s he returned to figurative painting, based on newspaper clippings. He has filled dozens of diaries with letters, but nobody knows what they're about. He is an inspiration to younger generations. He's represented by Knoll Gallery.

352 ATTILA SZŰCS
1967-

This soft-spoken, hard-working painter often uses unorthodox colours. His work often deals with the concept of time, in several ways. He takes his subjects from photos, random pictures from the internet, or from the collective memory. He works on canvasses, no matter how much time it takes. His paintings are said to evolve while being painted and even afterwards, in the showrooms.

353 PÉTER KORNISS
1937-
webdesign.hu/pkorniss

The *éminence grise* of Hungarian photography worked as a photo journalist for decades. He spent a lot of time in Transylvania in the 1960s to document life and traditions there, and he also followed the disintegration of that traditional way of life. He made a dozen photo books and is a respected member of juries. He never misses a vernissage or a chance to help someone.

354 BOLDI
1970-
sculptor.hu

Boldi is a popular, mainstream sculptor, whose work speaks to the man in the street. His sculptures emanate fun, but a peaceful, contemplative sort of fun. He has a special knack for creating public art. His statues *Scooter Boy* and *Sole*, both to be found in downtown Budapest, often make people stop and smile. He is a regular exhibitor abroad.

355 GÁBOR MIKLÓS SZŐKE
1987-
gabormiklosszoke.com

This artist is best known for his monumental animal sculptures; he has a feel for anatomy and large sizes. In the beginning of his career he created horses, whales and dogs out of coloured scrap wood. Later on he erected a huge chromium eagle in front of a stadium in Budapest, which led to a commission for the Atlanta Falcons baseball team: he created a giant falcon that's now standing in front of their stadium.

The 5 best places to enjoy
CLASSICAL MUSIC

---

356 MUSIC ACADEMY SOLTI HALL
VI. Liszt Ferenc tér 2.
Terézváros ⑦
+36 1 462 4600
zeneakademia.hu

For many people, the Music Academy is a synonym for the Grand Hall. But don't be fooled: the Small Hall, *Solti Terem* in Hungarian, is an equally interesting venue since it underwent a reconstruction in 2013. It's the ideal place to enjoy chamber music and small-scale opera productions. From any of the 330 seats the stage feels very near. The grey panelling is nice, as are the original chandeliers that are finally back where they belong.

357 OLD MUSIC ACADEMY
VI. Vörösmarty
utca 35.
Terézváros ⑦
+36 1 322 9804
lfze.hu

This 1879 building was erected for the Music Academy, which operated here until 1907. Liszt used to come here on foot from his apartment. The concert hall is on the first floor; most Saturdays there are free concerts at 11 am.

358 FUGA CENTER OF ARCHITECTURE

V. Petőfi Sándor utca 5.
Belváros ①
+36 1 266 2395
fuga.org.hu

Budapest architects traditionally love music. That's why their chamber's exhibition space and community centre regularly hosts concerts, on Sundays at 6 pm. The programming focusses on 20th and 21st-century music for piano or small formations, often performed by up-and-coming artists. Premieres for Hungary aren't uncommon.

359 MUSIC CONCERTS IN A CHURCH

muzsikalendarium.hu

Many Budapest churches have an interesting and rich concert programme, not necessarily related to liturgy. This calendar gives you an overview of the concerts that take place in town on a given day, seven days in advance. *Budapestfreeevents.com* tells you about free concerts. Most churches are heated in winter nowadays, but avoid surprises and find out first.

360 ÓBUDAI TÁRSASKÖR

III. Kiskorona utca 7.
Óbuda ⑲
+36 1 250 0288
obudaitarsaskor.hu

This classicist building in the heart of the Krúdy Quarter houses a much-loved music centre. It's one of the few fin de siècle buildings you'll spot there, flanked by a museum and a legendary restaurant. It has a 200-seat concert hall and is home to a string quartet, two chamber orchestras, and a ragtime band.

The 5 best venues for
LIVE JAZZ MUSIC

---

361 NOTHIN' BUT THE BLUES PUB

VIII. Krúdy Gyula utca 6.

Józsefváros ⑥

+36 20 322 8602

This pub is a local institution in a neighbourhood called the Magnates' Quarter, on the border of Budapest Soho. Since its opening in 1993, owner Csaba Posztós has been expanding the place and upgrading the furniture. The most recent addition is the adjacent wine cellar.

362 IF JAZZ CAFÉ

IX. Ráday utca 19.

Ferencváros ⑥

+36 1 299 0694

ifkavezo.hu

'You will like iF, iff you come in', says their slogan. They also boast that they are the place where you'll hear the best jazz in town. You'll find this pleasant split-level place in Budapest Soho's main street. In any case they offer the most chances to up-and-coming young artists nobody has heard about – yet.

363 BUDAPEST JAZZ CLUB

XIII. Hollán Ernő utca 7.

Újlipótváros ⑨

+36 1 798 7289

bjc.hu

Housed in a former cinema off Grand Boulevard, near Margaret Bridge, this is one of the most important venues of the expanding Budapest jazz scene. The cafe is open from 10 am onwards, and the concerts start at 8 pm. Check the website for the free jam sessions at 10.30 pm. Bistro food available.

364 OPUS JAZZ CLUB

IX. Mátyás utca 8.
Ferencváros ⑥
+36 1 216 7894
opusjazzclub.hu

In the unique Budapest Music Center complex you'll find this quality restaurant-and-club-in-one. It's thé place to hear local and visiting jazz bands, with occasional free concerts by up-and-coming ensembles. If you arrive early, ask the receptionist for a peek into the concert hall – it's the covered courtyard of a spice merchant's warehouse from the 1880s.

365 CAFÉ JEDERMANN

IX. Ráday utca 58.
Ferencváros ⑥
+36 30 406 3617
jedermann.hu

This cafe and informal jazz concert venue is on the ground floor of the Goethe Institut Budapest: they moved here after rising rents forced them out of Andrássy út. Usually there is a small entrance fee. Every Monday, at 8 pm, Kristóf Darvas plays the piano. He is an unclassifiable Budapest music sensation with phenomenal improvisation skills.

363 BUDAPEST JAZZ CLUB

The 5 most interesting places for
JEWISH HERITAGE

---

366 ORTHODOX SYNAGOGUE

**VII. Kazinczy
utca 29–31.
Erzsébetváros** ⑦
+36 1 351 0524
*kazinczyutcaiz
sinagoga.hu*

The hardcore traditional Jews of Hungary built their own synagogue here in 1911-13. It's an architectural delight, a rare example of early Hungarian Modernism. In his plans for the façade, the architect skilfully solved the problem caused by the bend in the street. The interior has a modernist structure adorned with Hungarian and Jewish folk motifs, a combination you won't see anywhere else.

367 MIKVEH

**VII. Kazinczy utca 16.
Erzsébetváros** ⑦
**+36 20 448 0164
(women)
+36 1 351 0524 (men)**
maoih.hu

In 2004, a Chassidic plumber from New York rebuilt this religious bath with his own hands; he worked here from Sunday to Thursday for months on end. The water comes from the cistern on the roof and from a newly driven well on site. To make sure the water was clean, they first poured 1000 litres of red wine in the well, and pumped it out.

368 HOLOCAUST MEMORIAL CENTER

IX. Páva utca 39.
Ferencváros ⑥
+36 1 455 3333
hdke.hu

The newly-built memorial centre – which was praised by Frank O. Gehry – incorporated a grand synagogue that had been underused. So a much smaller synagogue was erected in the corner of the building. It lacks the 100-year-old atmosphere and (maybe consequently) is more frequently open to visitors. They pray with a Sephardic accent.

369 YIDDISHE MAMMA MIA RESTAURANT

VII. Király utca 13.
Erzsébetváros ⑦
+36 1 878 1377
ymmrestaurant.com

Deep inside Budapest's nightlife mecca, called Gozsdu Arcade, you'll find this place, the dream-come-true of restaurateur Ferenc Salai. He was in love with both Jewish and Italian cuisine. The culinary team succeeds in combining the spices and the top recipes of these two separate worlds. The result isn't for weight watchers. Live music.

370 HUNGARIAN JEWISH MUSEUM AND ARCHIVES – RESEARCH ROOM

VII. Wesselényi utca 7.
Erzsébetváros ⑦
+36 1 413 5547
milev.hu

Once an old-time institution, now a state-of-the art, fully-digitalised centre at the disposal of anyone looking for their family roots, thanks to the smiling, workaholic historian Zsuzsa Toronyi. In the mid-2010s the archives were merged with the Jewish Museum, and the permanent exhibition was rearranged.

5 great
CONTEMPORARY STATUES

---

371 MEMORIAL OF THE 1956 REVOLUTION
XIV. Dózsa György út / Városligeti fasor Városliget ⑧

The design of this memorial for the 50th anniversary of the Revolution was chosen from over 70 proposals. It's a conceptual and physical work that speaks to the man in the street. It symbolises the power of united strength: it can even break up the pavement.

372 SCOOTER BOY
Corner of V. Duna utca and Váci utca Belváros ①

This friendly little granite statue stands at a busy crossroads. It looks inviting to touch, and you'll likely start scrutinising it. At second glance you'll realise that the boy is looking at the sky, and that his bike is impossible to ride. No one would know how to handle it, but that doesn't matter of course, it will stay here, like this, for ever.

373 'SHOES' MEMORIAL
Near Parliament, Danube Embankment Lipótváros ②

This often-documented classic memorial is the idea of a poet and his friend, a sculptor. It commemorates the Jewish Hungarians who were escorted by Hungarian Nazis and then shot into the icy river. Before, invariably, they were ordered to step out of their shoes.

374 GABOR SZTEHLO, LUTHERAN PASTOR

V. Deák Ferenc tér 12.
Belváros ①

Gabor Sztehlo was a Lutheran pastor (1909-1974) who saved the lives of about 2000 persecuted Jewish Hungarians, most of them children, whose parents never returned. This impressive monument by Tamas Vigh shows different aspects when viewed from different angles: bravery, energy, dedication, and from one side you can see the figure hides a child.

375 PLOT 301 MEMORIAL

AT: RÁKOSKERESZTÚR
CEMETERY / NEW
PUBLIC CEMETERY
X. Kozma utca 8.
Kőbánya
+36 1 433 7300

This was the site where the executed heroes of the revolution were buried, many of them with their faces turned down. Conceptualist artist György Jovánovics won the design contest and built a unique memorial, with a marble rod in the middle, which is exactly 1956 millimetres high. (The height was authenticated by the National Measurement Authority!)

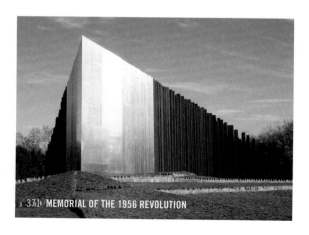

371 MEMORIAL OF THE 1956 REVOLUTION

5 *not-to-miss*
FESTIVALS

---

376 CAFE BUDAPEST CONTEMPORARY ART FESTIVAL
MID OCTOBER
+36 1 555 3000
cafebudapestfest.hu

Two weeks, three weekends, and a lot to do! Year after year the programme becomes more and more extensive – a snowball effect. Currently more than 40 venues partake in the festival, hosting over 250 shows and performances. As most new initiatives in Budapest, this festival takes place in October (in the hope of getting some public funding). Anyway, October is a great time to come to Budapest.

377 TITANIC FILM FESTIVAL
SECOND WEEK OF APRIL
titanicfilmfest.hu

This festival has been taking place every year since 1992. It's an excellent opportunity to discover gems that before didn't get the attention they deserve, of neither the mainstream nor the niche distributors. There are six sections, for example 'Asian Winds' or 'American Indies', and a competition. The centre of it all is the lavish Uránia cinema, but there are other venues as well, like club-like Toldi.

378 SZIGET FESTIVAL

EARLY AUGUST
**+36 20 345 9155
(during the festival)**
Óbuda ⑩
sziget.hu/fesztival

Sziget means 'island' – you can come to this music festival by boat on the river, which of course adds some charm to it all. It's a huge event that attracts tens of thousands of foreign youngsters. The programme features famous international bands as well as up-and-coming musicians, playing all kinds of music, plus a series of socially-conscious events dealing with for example the environment. You can sleep in your own tent.

379 BUDAPEST100 FESTIVAL

THE NEAREST WEEKEND
TO THE 100TH DAY
OF THE YEAR
budapest100.hu

This is an annual festival in honour of all the buildings in town that are exactly 100 years old in the year of celebration. The owners of those buildings open them to the public. After 2014 the festival temporarily deviated from the centenary concept, because hardly anything was built during WWI; they then celebrated the embankments, Grand Boulevard, etc. The organising committee plans to return to the original idea around 2020.

380 FESTIVAL ACADEMY BUDAPEST

JUNE OR JULY
fesztivalakademia.hu

Artistic directors Barnabás Kelemen and Katalin Kokas initiated this lovely, small-scale, one-week midsummer chamber music festival at the Music Academy. Apart from concerts there are lectures, master courses and other music-related events. The Vigadó Concert Hall is also one of the venues.

GELLÉRT HILL SLIDE PARK

25 THINGS TO DO WITH CHILDREN

The 5 best places to

TAKE THE LITTLE ONES

381 MINIVERSUM

VI. Andrássy út 12.
Terézváros ⑦
miniversum.hu

With its 100 trains on 1300 metres of track, this privately-owned exhibition is an amazing place, displaying 14 miniature cities, populated by 5000 figures. There are interactive elements throughout, and you walk through the stationmasters' room too. On the walls there are stories about Hungarian history. A treat for all ages!

382 CHILDREN'S RAILWAY

XII. Széchenyi
hegy – Hűvösvölgy
Hegyvidék ⑪
+36 1 397 5394
gyermekvasut.hu

This 11,2-kilometre-long narrow and steep rail line was built after the Soviet model, but despite that it was – and still is – very popular. Apart from the driving, everything is taken care of by 10 to 14 year-old kids. It takes 45 minutes to go 235 metres up or down. In 1990 the ideological names of the stops were all changed.

383 BUDAPEST PUPPET THEATRE

VI. Andrássy út 69.
Terézváros ⑦
+36 1 342 2702
budapest-babszinhaz.hu

Their slogan is: 'A theatre where a puppet isn't only for kids; it's a genre'. This puppet theatre is the biggest in Central Europe. It has 403 seats in the big room, and 99 in the smaller room. It is a municipally-owned, professional repertory theatre.

384 CAPITAL CIRCUS OF BUDAPEST

XIV. Állatkerti
körút 12/a.
Zugló ⑧
+36 1 343 8300
fnc.hu

The smell of animals is always lingering in this huge state-owned circus, which was built in the communist era. The current director is experimenting with blending circus and classic, theatre-type storytelling. 'New Circus' (a widely successful genre in Budapest) shows aren't on the programme. Every second January the International Circus Festival takes place here.

385 AQUAWORLD

IV. Íves út 16.
Újpest
+36 1 231 3760
aquaworldresort.hu

It isn't central, but Aquaworld has enough to offer for a full day outing. Under a huge, transparent dome you'll find a dozen pools, and 11 different waterslides. In summer a beach part is added. There is a Sauna World section – with an extra admission fee. You pay for everything with your watch-like plastic gadget.

381 MINIVERSUM

5

PLAYGROUNDS
for lots of fun

---

386 **9 MAY PARK**

III. Hajógyári sziget
Óbuda ⑩

On the island that's known as the location of the Sziget Festival you'll find this very large, hilly playground, known and loved by kids because of its slides. There are two metal-tube-slides, with peaks in little towers, for parent-kid combos. There are smaller, open slides as well, and also ropes and rolling discs.

387 **ELEVENPARK**

XI. Hengermalom
út 19–21.
Újbuda ⑤
+36 1 203 3022
elevenpark.hu

The name is a pun: in Hungarian it means 'lively', in English it is a hint to the district number. It is a 4000-square-metres indoor cross between a funfair, an adventure park and a playground, with all kinds of known and never-heard-of gadgets that can free even the liveliest kids of their extra energy.

388 GELLÉRT HILL SLIDE PARK

South slope of
Gellért Hill
Újbuda ⑤

When this playground was upgraded in 2017, a large part of the hill slope was covered with rubber, to make it safe for kids. There are slides, rope variations (vertical and horizontal) and small bumps for toddlers to mount. An effort was made to entertain larger families with kids of various ages. Accessible from Szent Gellért tér.

389 MÉSZKŐ PARK

III. Mészkő utca
Óbuda ⑩

This playground was built on a former illegal dump, after pressure from a local NGO. It turned out to be a really pleasant place with traditional kids' stuff, plus room to play basketball and table tennis, and wooden towers resembling pirate outposts, with built-in telescopes. Take some food with you, there aren't any shops nearby.

390 MARGARET ISLAND

Between Buda
and Pest ⑨

In 2017 Margaret Island got its latest facelift. There are three major playgrounds, as well as other child-friendly amusement like a small (free) petting zoo, a large rose garden, a programmed fountain, and a large patch of grass, which was used for playing polo in the interwar period, and now is great for playing frisbee.

The 5 cutest
SHOPS FOR KIDS

---

391 KAMORKA

XIII. Pozsonyi út 20.
Újlipótváros ⑨
+36 20 957 9115
kamorka.hu

This is a 100% 'green' kidswear brand; they insist on chemical-free and locally-made raw materials and the smallest possible carbon print. They only use materials made in Hungary, and they also work according to fair-trade principles. Even the sheep that supply the wool for Kamorka are fed with organic food only.

392 GINGER BROWNIE

V. Váci utca 49.
1st Fl.
Belváros ①
gingerbrownie.com

This niche brand designs quality dresses for girls aged 2 to 9 – the age group that's likely to want to look like little princesses, or to dress up like their mothers. The design team pays close attention to the materials they work with, so that the dresses don't just look nice, but also feel comfortable and pleasant to wear.

393 MINIPOLISZ

VI. Király utca 8–10.
Central Passage
1st Fl.
Terézváros ⑦
+36 30 584 6626
minipolisz.hu

'A place where you can be an adult for once' – a sort of genuine infotainment centre, where kids can dress up and try out different jobs: a shop or a petrol station assistant for example, or a cashier, a policeman, a prison guard, a doctor, and so on.

394 PAGONY

XI. Bartók Béla út 5.
Újbuda ⑤
+36 1 794 3719
bartok.pagony.hu

This large book, toy and boardgame shop near Szent Gellért tér is sort of a quality activity centre for kids. It's a very cosy, special place, where one would start to think that sales are only secondary. They regularly host book launches, of their own as well as of other publications. The staff is very knowledgeable. They have an older sister shop of the same name in Pest.

395 PICI AND THE CITY

I. Mikó utca 1.
1st Fl.
Krisztinaváros ③
+36 20 218 2654
piciandthecity.com

This showroom is the brainchild of a young mother and DIY blogger. She was looking for T-shirts, coats, shoes, etc. for her baby and toddler, with nice colours and of good quality, so that they wouldn't wear out so easily, but they turned out to be pretty hard to find. And that's why she decided to create her own business, specialised in that niche.

394 PAGONY

The 5 best
MUSEUMS FOR KIDS

---

396 PALACE OF WONDERS (CSOPA)

III. Bécsi út 38–42
Óbuda ⑩
+36 1 814 8060
csopa.hu

This is a large – two levels, about 5000 square metres – privately-run science showroom and playhouse. They constantly improve and increase the number of experiments you can follow – there are about 250 of them now. They moved to their present location in 2017. Great fun for adults, too.

397 BUDAPEST ZOO

XIV. Állatkerti körút 6–12.
Zugló ⑧
+36 1 273 4900
zoobudapest.com

This is a unique zoo and botanical garden, with some amazing art nouveau pavilions, built before WWI. Two artificial cliffs enlarge the site. A great place to start your visit is the lookout tower of the elephant house. They're planning to add a huge 'biodome' with a subtropical climate soon.

398 HUNGARIAN RAILWAY HISTORY PARK

XIV. Tatai út 95.
Zugló ⑧
+36 1 450 1497
vasuttortenetipark.hu

This museum was opened in 2000, in a building that was no longer used by the national railway company. It is a mecca for locomotive-loving kids. You can see and touch a great many of them, you can even travel on some of them on an 800-metre-long track. Twenty-nine types of steam locomotives on the site!

399 MESEMÚZEUM / FAIRY TALE MUSEUM

I. Döbrentei utca 15.
Víziváros ④
+36 1 202 4020
mesemuzeum.hu

Right after entering this 200-year-old building you'll bump into a large dollhouse, in which the building's story is told in the form of fully-furnished microscopic rooms. Hungarian fairy tales tend to follow common European patterns, so foreign kids will not have too much difficulty to understand the ones that are told here.

400 TROPICARIUM

XXII. Nagytétényi út 37–43.
Budatétény ⑤
+36 1 424 3053
tropicarium.hu

This is a zoo with sharks. Like in a theatre, the experience builds up: first you get to see a great many Hungarian fish, then a rain forest with its animals, and so on, until you finally reach the 11-metre-long transparent tunnel where the sharks swim above your head. They are fed before the eyes of the visitors every Thursday at 3 pm.

5
CHILD-FRIENDLY
cafes and restaurants

401 CAFÉ MAGNET

V. Balassi Bálint
utca 9–11.
Lipótváros ②
+36 1 428 8808
magnetbank.hu

Named after the small 'community bank' that has an office in this building on the Pest river front. The cafe basically caters to waiting customers but also to passers-by. There's a corner for babies and toddlers, that's quite well-equipped with toys, a blackboard to draw on, and books for older kids.

402 NÁNCSI NÉNI VENDÉGLŐJE

II. Ördögárok út 80.
Hegyvidék ⑪
+36 1 397 2742
nancsineni.hu

'Aunt Lucy's Inn' is a popular Buda establishment in a former farmhouse, in a wealthy neighbourhood, about 20 minutes from downtown. It has been serving traditional Hungarian and French cuisine since 1980. The portions are big and mouth-watering, and it's an ideal place for family events. If you've left your glasses at home, they'll offer you a pair, so that you can closely examine the long menu.

403 REMÍZ CAFÉ AND RESTAURANT

II. Budakeszi út 5.
Hegyvidék ⑪
+36 30 999 5131
remiz.hu

Remíz (depot in English) is next door to
an actual tram depot. It's a much-liked
Buda place, a favourite of Buda celebrities,
run by the first and second generation
of the Meződi family. They offer very
traditional courses and some moderately
innovative ones. There's lots of room, and
the terrace is an especially pleasant place
to sit, weather permitting.

404 PASTRAMI

III. Lajos utca 93–99.
Óbuda ⑩
+36 1 430 1731
pastrami.hu

A large, trendy, 21st-century restaurant
with a sleek industrial design, which is
in contrast with the funny, heart-dictated
details and the open kitchen. The food
is somewhere halfway between bistro-
quality and more ambitious cuisine. It
attracts different kinds of customers
depending on the time of day, and in
the weekend, this is a family-place. The
website provides a glossary to help you
fully understand the menu.

405 SOPHIE & BEN

VI. Káldy Gyula
utca 5.
Terézváros ⑦
+36 30 208 7700
sophieben.hu

This place, named after the owners' twins,
is in the heart of the nightlife district.
It offers organic burgers, pulled pork
burger, and bistro dishes, as well as homemade pastries and special craft beers.
There is a kids' menu and a play area.

BRODY HOUSE

30 PLACES
TO SLEEP

The 5 best places to
SLEEP NEXT TO THE WATER

406 ART'OTEL

I. Bem rakpart 16–19.
Víziváros ④
+36 1 487 9487
artotels.com

This hotel is housed in a number of historic 18th-century buildings on the Buda river front, to which a new façade was added during the renovation. It's part of a German chain with a strong concept: for every hotel they choose an artist, whose work is exhibited in the rooms, in common spaces, even on the plates. In Budapest it's Donald Sultan (1951), an American painter, sculptor and print maker.

407 THE CLARK

I. Clark Ádám tér 1.
Víziváros ④
+36 1 610 4890
theclark.hu

This is where you'll find the best possible river view, from any of the 86 rooms. Hotel The Clark was built on a bomb site that had remained vacant for quite some time after the war. Several ideas and designs for new buildings were proposed, and criticised. This building, by the Australian immigrant architect Anthony Gall, was also criticised online – some people always seem to know better.

408 LÁNCHÍD 19 DESIGN HOTEL BUDAPEST

I. Lánchíd utca 19.
Víziváros ④
+36 1 457 1200
lanchid19hotel.com

A perfect blend of old and new. The building houses a medieval watermill in the cellar, and at the same time boasts an extraordinary changing glass façade, which is brilliantly illuminated at night. The hotel won several design awards and offers four-star comfort along with great design solutions in every corner. There are 45 rooms and 3 panorama suites.

409 DANUBIUS HOTEL GELLÉRT

XI. Szent Gellért tér 2.
Újbuda ⑤
+36 1 889 5500
danubiushotels.com

This very large hotel was built in 1918 and became the hallmark of Budapest high-end hospitality during the interwar period. The complex includes a wonderful art nouveau swimming pool and open-air baths, connected to the hotel building. The baths have already been given a facelift, the hotel is badly in need of one. Insist on a discount.

410 IBIS STYLES BUDAPEST CITY HOTEL

IX. Soroksári út 12.
Ferencváros ⑥
+36 1 455 8300
ibis.com

Located on the less elegant end of Grand Boulevard, this affordable three-star hotel looks out on the A38 concert hall on the other side of the river. It's a great place to stay for classical music buffs, as it is close to the Bartok Concert hall. Throughout the building you'll bump into a 'bicycle' theme.

5 of the nicest
BOUTIQUE HOTELS

411 SOHO HOTEL

VII. Dohány utca 64.
Erzsébetváros ⑦
+36 1 872 8292
sohoboutiquehotel.com

A small and (dog-)friendly design hotel of the affordable kind, very near Café New York and the nightlife district. It's a perfect place for the discovery-minded and fans of the urban jungle. There's an underground parking space, and two suites offer extra facilities (like a bathtub). Free for kids aged under 6.

412 BALTAZÁR

I. Országház utca 31.
Várnegyed ④
+36 1 300 7051
baltazarbudapest.com

A unique place, partly in an old building and partly in a new extension. There are 11 colourful rooms and suites, each one with a different, unique and somewhat bohemian design, furnished with a tasteful and original mix of vintage and modern pieces. Baltazár Grill is also a celebrated bistro in its own right.

413 LA PRIMA FASHION HOTEL

V. Piarista utca 6.
Belváros ①
+36 1 799 0088
laprimahotel
budapest.com

This centrally located four-star hotel has 80 rooms, including some suites, some interconnected rooms, and also a room especially equipped for guests in wheelchairs. The hotel also offers high-tech conference facilities and a fitness room.

414 HOTEL MOMENTS

VI. Andrássy út 8.
Terézváros ⑦
+36 1 611 7000
hotelmoments
budapest.hu

This mid-size, immaculately designed and renovated hotel is housed in a historic palace from the 1880s. The location is pure magic: it's on the nicest avenue in town, between the Cathedral and the Opera House. The loft rooms offer panoramic views. Breakfast is superb. It's served in the Bistro Fine, which is a fine restaurant for lunch and dinner as well.

415 ARIA HOTEL

V. Hercegprímás
utca 5.
Lipótváros ②
+36 1 445 4055
ariahotelbudapest.com

This hotel is unlike any other, thanks to the four wings that are dedicated to four different musical genres: classical, opera, contemporary music and jazz. Great features are the roof bar with its panoramic view and the sophisticated spa. In the late afternoon guests are offered a selection of Hungarian wines and cheeses for free.

414 HOTEL MOMENTS

The 5 best
APARTMENTS WITH A VIEW

416 BEDŐ HOUSE APARTMENT

V. Honvéd utca 3.
Lipótváros ②
bblaccommodation.com

A high-end, two-storey penthouse apartment, on the top two floors of an art nouveau building from 1903, called the Bedö House. Up to seven guests can sleep here in five bedrooms, with '2,5' bathrooms available. The tower living room offers a spectacular, almost-360-degrees view. It's a nice blend of modern facilities and a historic setting.

417 BASILICA APARTMENT

V. Bajcsy Zsilinszky út 19.
Terézváros ⑦
airbnb.hu/
rooms/19674072

Located only 200 metres from the cathedral, this apartment offers a perfect view on the dome from the balcony. It's on the fifth floor of a classic 1930s apartment block and ideal for two persons. The location is very convenient: it's close to downtown Budapest as well as to the Opera House, and some of the top restaurants are within walking distance.

418 PAULAY HOUSE APARTMENTS

VI. Paulay Ede utca 16.
Belváros ②
+36 1 266 1211
brody.land/
brody-apartments

The BrodyLand concept consists of a design hotel, a club and these apartments. They can be rented for a short or a long term, and guests are welcome in the club. The rooms are furnished in the 'BrodyLand style': a contemporary design, skilfully mixed with vintage furniture.

419 LARGE DESIGNER HOME WITH BALCONY

Terézváros ⑦
airbnb.nl/
rooms/11163475

This 135-square-metre apartment with high ceilings has two bedrooms and two large living rooms. It is situated on top of a classic apartment block, between the old-fashioned Király utca and the glitzy Andrássy út, and very close to the House of Terror. Every single review gives this apartment five stars. Great public transport connections.

420 SPACIOUS ROOFTOP TERRACED 2-BEDROOM CITY APARTMENT

Near the Opera
Terézváros ⑦
Search tripadvisor.
co.uk for the definition
'Spacious Rooftop
Terraced 2 Bedroom
City Apartment'
Budapest

Situated on top of a traditional apartment block on Andrássy út, the flat overlooks a side street at the back. Two large bedrooms, two bathrooms and an extra-large balcony, from where you can see the rooftop of the Opera House; fits a maximum of five people. The owner will welcome you personally and will show you around the neighbourhood if you like.

5

HOTELS WITH
A HISTORY

421 DANUBIUS HOTEL ASTORIA

V. Kossuth Lajos
utca 19.
Belváros ①
+36 1 889 6000
danubiushotels.com

This very elegant hotel was built here in the early 20th century, on the site where there used to be a city gate. It was in this very hotel, in a small conference room, that the National Council convened and declared Hungary a republic. It is now a three-star hotel, with a nice in-house cafe, awaiting renovation.

422 HOTEL PALAZZO ZICHY

VIII. Lőrinc pap
tér 2.
Józsefváros ⑥
+36 1 235 4000
hotel-palazzo-zichy.hu

This fancy design hotel with 80 rooms opened in 2009. The neo-baroque style building was built in 1899 for Count Nándor Zichy (1829-1911), a politician and member of parliament. During the communist era it was nationalised and divided into apartments. The neighbourhood is called the Palace District and is close to the National Museum.

423 CORINTHIA HOTEL BUDAPEST

VII. Erzsébet
körút 43–49.
Erzsébetváros ⑦
+36 1 479 4000
corinthia.com

When this hotel was built in 1896, it was the biggest and fanciest hotel of the Austro-Hungarian monarchy. It boasts a huge ballroom, which was converted into the Red Star cinema in the 1950s. The renovation to make the hotel meet modern standards was completed in 2003, and included the installation of a spacious 1000-square-metre spa and fitness. Corinthia Hotel Budapest is on Grand Boulevard, near the Music Academy.

424 CONTINENTAL HOTEL ZARA BUDAPEST

VII. Dohány
utca 42–44.
Erzsébetváros ⑦
+36 1 815 1000
continentalhotel
budapest.com

This large hotel with 272 rooms (including 13 suites) opened in 2010. The Art Nouveau-style reception area used to be part of a grandiose art nouveau bath house that closed in 1970 – Hungária Bath (1910-1970). Now the wellness and fitness facilities are on the top floor. From April to September you can use the rooftop swimming pool.

425 MAISON BUDAPEST

I. Országház utca 17.
Várnegyed ④
+36 1 405 4980
maisonbudapest.hu

A lovely, quiet hotel in the historic Castle District. It was a cooper's workshop in the late Middle Ages, after that is was the home and workshop of the Spiegel bakers for several centuries. The present hotel, with 17 rooms (including two suites) with a unique design opened in 2017. It has a very deep cellar, where breakfast is served and events take place.

5 wonderful
SMALL HOTELS

426 GERLÓCZY ROOMS DE LUX

V. Gerlóczy utca 1.
Belváros ①
+36 1 501 4000
gerloczy.hu/rooms

There's no foyer, that's why this place isn't called a hotel. It's very centrally located, yet it's very quiet. It has a bistro restaurant downstairs, also called Gerlóczy, after the first mayor of unified Budapest. There are only 19 rooms, four of which are in the attic. Probably best price/quality ratio in the Budapest hotel scene.

427 CASATI BUDAPEST HOTEL

VI. Paulay Ede
utca 31.
Terézváros ⑦
+36 1 343 1198
casatibudapesthotel.hu

Behind the 18th-century façade you'll find this friendly 25-room boutique hotel, with lots of contemporary design elements. The rooms fall into four categories: Classic, Cool, Natural and Heaven. There are original paintings in all rooms. Kids under 14 aren't allowed. The building also houses the Tuk Tuk Bar, one of the best bars in town. Close to the Opera House.

428 HOTEL MIKA SUPERIOR

VII. Kazinczy utca 47.
Erzsébetváros ⑦
+36 30 194 6568
hotelmika.com

Tivadar Mika was a coppersmith who opened a factory here in 1907. 110 years later, the factory building was converted into this three-star hotel with 12 rooms. It's the brainchild of a group of young entrepreneurs, who believe in the potential of a small hotel right in the centre of the nightlife district. Onsite they also run Mika Tivadar Mulato pub and club.

429 LAVENDER CIRCUS HOSTEL

V. Múzeum körót 37.,
doorbell 9
Belváros ①
+36 70 417 7763
lavendercircus.com

A very quiet, secret place, with 15 double rooms, seven of which have an en suite bathroom. The owner, Bohemian artist Szarvas, decorated all the rooms with his drawings, giving every room its own unique look. There's no breakfast service, but guests can use the kitchen. There's no lift either, but younger and perfectly fit people won't mind.

430 OPERA-GARDEN HOTEL

V. Hajós utca 24.
Terézváros ⑦
+36 1 301 9030
operagardenhotel.hu

To create this hotel, an extra storey was added on top of a two-storey art nouveau block of flats – the addition clearly contrasts with the original part because of the dark metal walls. The hotel has 35 rooms, all with a separate kitchen area, including a dining table. The rooms on the top floor are decorated in a rougher style, and can be reached through a private access by stairs.

The 5 most
ECCENTRIC HOTELS

431 BRODY HOUSE

VIII. Bródy Sándor
utca 10.
Józsefváros ① ⑥
+36 1 266 1211
brody.land

This eccentric 11-room hotel is filled to the brim with works of art. The rooms are named after artists who either stayed here or collaborated with the two British owners. These named their hotel after Hungarian writer Sandor Brody, who also gave his name to the street. Opposite Brody House is the garden of the National Museum.

432 KŐLEVES FOGADÓ

VII. Kazinczy utca 41.
Erzsébetváros ⑦
+36 1 322 1011
kolevesvendeglo.hu

Located behind the restaurant with the same name. You can choose to stay in one of three very different spaces: the Studio, the Quadruple Room, or Room No. 3. The building is right in the middle of the nightlife district, and is close to three metro lines.

433 HOTEL RUM

V. Királyi Pál utca 4.
Belváros ①
+36 1 424 9060
hotelrumbudapest.com

A highly original boutique hotel, specifically designed by an all-Hungarian team for 'modern urban explorers'. It has 38 rooms; they fall into four categories and are 15 to 30 square metres large. There's a fantastic roof bar, and also a celebrated Asian restaurant called Urban Tiger.

434 **BOHEM ART HOTEL**

V. Molnár utca 35.
Belváros ①
+36 1 327 9020
bohemarthotel.hu

This small hotel in the historic city centre claims to combine the best features of design and hip hotels. It takes up the two storeys of a former stationery factory; the four upper-floors were added later on. The rooms are a bit on the small side, but packed with the art of emerging Hungarian artists. A gay-friendly hotel.

435 **THE HIVE PARTY HOSTEL**

VII. Dob utca 19.
Erzsébetváros ⑦
+36 30 826 6197
thehive.hu

This meticulously restored old building houses an improbable 21st-century youth hostel. It resembles the inside of a spaceship, with about 300 all-white comfortable bunk beds, and toilets that look as if they were made for a four-star hotel. You don't need to leave the premises to enjoy a ruin bar: there is one in-house!

431 BRODY HOUSE

SZÉCHENYI BATH

25 ACTIVITIES FOR THE WEEKEND

5 nice
DAY TRIPS

---

436 SZENTENDRE

It takes 30 minutes by car or commuter train to get to this charming little 18th-century town north of Budapest, along the Danube. A former artists colony, it has great museums around the main square. Climb the hill to gaze at the half a dozen church spires; it's worth the effort.

437 NORTH OF LAKE BALATON

The dozen villages on the slopes of these hills are inhabited by thousands of intellectuals and business people who modernised old peasant mansions and added new villas. They patronise great wine cellars and some of the best restaurants in the country, and know which beaches to visit. Two hours by car from the city.

438 KECSKEMÉT

One hour by car from Budapest, this typical south-east small town has a great main square with a giant art nouveau town hall, and other fine buildings. You can eat some great food here, mainly traditional Hungarian cuisine, fit for the shepherds who are in the fields 7/7 for weeks. There's also a great photo museum in a small, former synagogue.

439 LAKE TISZA

Ninety minutes by car from Budapest, in the north-east of Hungary, you'll see this artificial pond. It was created by a dam in 1973 and it's a great place for nature lovers and bird watchers. You can rent rooms, boats, guides and bikes in the half a dozen small villages around the lake. Look for the Ecocentre in a village called Poroszló.

440 PÉCS

Two hours by car or train, this small town in the south of the country has a Mediterranean feel to it. It has many museums, and it's home to quite a number of students. There's a nice, well-kept main square, and a wonderful music hall completed in 2011 – the music scene here alone is worth the trip. There is also a cool and interesting cultural centre in a working china and porcelain manufactory called Zsolnay.

The 5
BEACHES (*STRAND*)
to visit in the Budapest area

---

441 PALATINUS STRAND

XIII. Margitsziget /
Margaret Island ⑨
+36 1 340 4500
palatinusstrand.hu

This beach in the middle of Margaret Island became popular during the interwar period, when Budapest first started realising how great an asset its situation by the water was (and still is). Since 2017 the beach is open all year round: the city added an indoor part, with ten pools (including a wave pool) and giant slides.

442 CSILLAGHEGYI STRAND

III. Pusztakúti út 2–6.
Óbuda ⑩
+36 1 242 0754
csillaghegyistrand.hu

The oldest city beach is a favourite among lovers of cold water. It is surrounded by a wonderful wooded park on a hillside. The pools are arranged in terraces. The 33-metre swimming pool is covered by a tent in winter. In 2018 a new fitness and wellness part was added.

443 LUPA PREMIUM BEACH (LUPA-TÓ)

Tó utca 1.
Budakalász
lupato.hu

A visionary businessman added this beach to the Budapest scene in 2016. The centre is a big former mining pond, with crystal-clear water and with facilities all around, including some of the best street food vendors. You can buy tickets in different categories, with services accordingly. A unique Budapest-only experience, just 20 minutes by car from the city centre.

444 KÜLKER PARK

II. Budakeszi út 73/c.
Hegyvidék ⑪
+36 1 200 1898
kulkerpark.hu

The peculiar name of this 'Foreign Trade Park' refers to its former owner: the communist-era Ministry of Foreign Trade. It's a lesser known, less crowded beach in the Buda Hills, with a professional Olympic pool, and tennis and volleyball grounds. It also offers a wall-climbing facility, and reasonable food for the day.

445 PASKÁL BATH

XIV. Egressy út 178/f.
Zugló ⑧
+36 1 252 6944
paskalfurdo.hu

This is the youngest beach in town – it was completed in 2016. It has ten pools, and offers a great variety of wellness and fitness services. There's an adventure pool with a bar, a sauna heated by geothermic energy, and an Ice'N'Go Pavilion. In eastern Pest, a fast-growing and gentrifying area.

The 5 best
CYCLING ROUTES

446 KOSSUTH SQUARE – ALKOTMÁNY UTCA – BAJCSY – ANDRÁSSY ÚT – CITY PARK

This is a perfect route to explore on a city bike. The bicycle-lane-only itinerary takes you along the most elegant parts of the city, and won't take longer than 30 minutes – which is how long you can use a city bike for free. One subscriber can use four bikes at a time.

447 BUDA RIVERBANK: FROM KOPASZI GÁT TO GRAPHISOFT PARK

This is quite a scenic route, taking you from one recent side of Budapest to the other one, crossing the historic city in between, with plenty of bridges to admire along the way. Be careful, Budapest people do not always respect bike lanes, especially on the riverbank.

448 AROUND MARGARET ISLAND

This bike ride takes no more than 15 minutes. The island is car-free, but there is a bus traversing it. You'll come across the petting zoo, some interesting ruins, including those of a nunnery where Princess Margaret was sent to: her father, King Béla IV, promised that sacrifice to God, if Mongol invaders would leave and not return. They did not.

449 MARGARET BRIDGE – BUDA TO NORTH – ARPAD BRIDGE – PEST TO SZABADSÁG BRIDGE – BUDA TO MARGARET BRIDGE

This route covers large chunks of the embankments, named after foreigners and Hungarians who risked their lives while saving the lives of Jewish Hungarians who were persecuted by the German and Hungarian Nazis in 1944-45. It's quite a scenic route, but be careful: don't forget to pay attention to the road while you're gazing at the other bank of the river.

450 BUBI BIKES

If you are a 'casual', i.e. non-permanent user, you can purchase a card from the touchscreen terminals at the docking stations. The card is valid for 24 or 72 hours, or a week. When purchasing a ticket, a deposit per bike is blocked on your bank account. Unblocking it might take up to 15 workdays.

450 BUBI BIKES

5 great
HIKING TOURS
in the Buda Hills

---

451 TRAILS OF BUDAPEST

+36 70 361 99 74
trailsofbudapest.com

This small, dedicated company offers daily hiking tours, taking 3, 4, 5 or 6 hours. Simply check in and go to the meeting point. The friendly, enthusiastic staff are very experienced. All the tours alternate between narrow trails and lookout spots.

452 ELIZABETH LOOKOUT TOWER, JÁNOS HILL

XII. János-hegy
Hegyvidék ⑪
+36 1 224 5900

Take the 21A bus from Széll Kálmán tér to the Normafa stop. From there you go for a half-hour walk that will lead you to the lookout tower, the highest point in Budapest. It is 23,5 metres high, with 100 steps leading to the top. In communist times a giant neon red star was attached to the tower.

453 LION'S ROCK – HÁRMASHATÁR HILL

III. Hármashatárhegyi út 1.
Hegyvidék ⑲ ⑪

The National Blue Hiking Path is a convenient trail for tourists who are in for a light hiking tour. Hármashatár Hill is situated between District II. and III., and its slopes are the headquarters of gliders and hang gliders. A popular destination is a large piece of dolomite called Lion Rock – it resembles a sitting lion.

454 PÁLVÖLGY CAVE / CAVE OF PAUL VALLEY

II. Szépvölgyi út 162.
Hegyvidék ⑪
+36 1 325 9505
dunaipoly.hu

This cave is 29 kilometres long, the longest one in Hungary. 500 metres of it can be visited during guided tours. You can reach the cave by taking the 65 bus, from the Kolosy tér terminus. There is a constant temperature of 11°C down there. Not for kids under 5 years or 105 centimetres.

455 NAGY-HÁRS HILL AND KAÁN KÁROLY LOOKOUT TOWER

This is one of the less crowded trails; there are no paved routes leading up to it. You can get off the Children's Railway at the Hárshegy stop and then go further up the hills. The tower there was named after Károly Kaán (1887-1940), a legendary forest engineer and state secretary who was responsible for forestry and introduced modern nature preservation policies in Hungary.

The 5 best
BATH HOUSES

---

456 **RUDAS BATH**

I. Döbrentei tér 9.
Víziváros ④
+36 1 356 1322
rudasfurdo.hu

A visit to this bath is a great experience. It consists of three distinct parts: an authentic Turkish bath, a 19th-century part, and a newly-built 21st-century wing in the south end. The latter comes with a splendid roof terrace and an open-air tub, a terrific place to spend a winter evening.

457 **SZÉCHENYI BATH**

XIV. Állatkerti körút 9–11.
Városliget ⑧
+36 1 363 3210
szechenyifurdo.hu

The biggest bath in Budapest, in City Park, was built in 1913 to accommodate people who did not have a bathroom at home, for their weekly wash. The open-air part was added in 1927, it was originally covered with sand, in imitation of a seaside beach. Now part of it is an adventure pool.

458 **DANDÁR BATH**

IX. Dandár utca 5–7.
Ferencváros ⑥
+36 1 215 7084
dandarfurdo.hu

This is the smallest bath in Budapest, built in art deco style and completed in 1936, to accommodate the inhabitants of the working class neighbourhood. The area is gentrifying fast these days and the bath, which was fully modernised in 2014–15, now attracts a younger crowd.

459 GELLÉRT THERMAL BATH

XI. Kelenhegyi út 4.
Újbuda ⑤
+36 1 466 6166
gellertfurdo.hu

The art nouveau bath in the Hotel Gellért emanates the splendour of the Good Old Days – especially the indoor part, which was meticulously renovated around 2000. The most popular item of the outdoor part is the wave pool. The bath is situated between the river and Gellért hill, the vicinity of the woods is palpable here.

460 IRGALMASOK VELI BEJ FÜRDŐJE

II. Árpád fejedelem utca 7.
Hegyvidék ⑨⑪
+36 1 438 8587
irgalmasrend.hu/site/ velibej

This is the oldest Turkish bath in town, it was first mentioned in 1584. Terribly neglected during the communist period, it was revived after 2000, when the hospital complex around it was given back to the religious order, whose mission was healing and curing. It opened in 2012, with five pools. It is a real secret for locals, too.

457 SZÉCHENYI BATH

BUDA CASTLE FUNICULAR

40 RANDOM FACTS AND URBAN DETAILS

The 5
ODDEST THINGS
about Budapest

---

461 PEST IS RISING

Looking from hilly Buda at Pest, the latter looks completely flat. Anyone who ever tried to bike from the river to Kőbánya or District X. knows that isn't true. Pest, as a matter of fact, is incrementally growing higher and higher, as it moves away from the Danube. Geologists compare it to an amphitheatre created by nature.

462 23 SEMI-INDEPENDENT FIEFDOMS

Budapest, a city of 1,7 million inhabitants, is highly compartmentalised; there are 23 districts, each with its own elected mayor and city council. There is a mayor-in-chief as well, but he has limited power. The coordination of the different districts is slow and difficult, and corruption is probably higher as a consequence of that.

463 A SPA CITY AND A BIG CITY AT THE SAME TIME

Budapest is a spa city, but a special one: usually spa cities are small settlements that have little to offer besides thermal water. Budapest has a lot of attractions; the baths are just one of them. The concept was first brought to Buda by the Turks. Until WWII there were about a dozen Danube swimming pools. These days Budapest baths are mostly used by families with kids, and tourists. Ordinary people go to fitness clubs and gyms with small pools.

464 CHAPEL IN THE ROCK
XI. Gellérthegy

The medieval-looking chapel was inaugurated in 1931. It has been carved into the south slope of Gellért Hill and serves as a place for prayers by the monks of the nearby monastery. It was brutally closed on Easter Monday 1951, when the monks were deported, and some of them killed. The chapel was reopened for the monks and the public in 1992.

465 AN EXACT COPY OF A FIRENZE PALACE

You could call Budapest a city of copies: many buildings will remind visitors of buildings in Vienna or Paris. Batthyány Palace for example (Teréz körút 13.) is a close to perfect copy of Palazzo Strozzi (1538), in Firenze. The copy was designed by Lajos Hauszmann, a leading architect of his time.

5 odd
TRANSPORT METHODS

---

466 COG-WHEEL RAILWAY
Between II. Szilágyi Erzsébet fasor and XII. Széchenyi hegy
③ ⑪

Officially called tram no. 60, this railway serves the Buda Hills; it was inaugurated in 1874. The cogs are in the middle, the fitting steel wheel helps to overcome the difference in height. Since 1926 it is powered by electricity. It has ten stops, the total travel time is about 20 minutes. The tram carries bicycles, too.

467 ZUGLIGET CHAIRLIFT
Between Zugliget and János Hill ⑪

This special vehicle in the 12th district covers 1040 metres in 15 minutes, spanning a level difference of 262 metres. It connects Zugliget and János Hill, the highest point in Budapest. It was launched in 1970. Its name, *libegő*, comes from the Hungarian word for floating.

468 THE OLDEST METRO ON THE CONTINENT
Between Vörösmarty tér and Mexikói út
① ⑧

The M1 metro line was built under Andrássy út in only 21 months. It opened in 1896, and was the second underground line in Europe. The lovely old carriages can still be seen today, in a small museum dedicated to that metro line. They stand on a piece of the original track, which was made redundant when line 2 opened.

469 BUDA CASTLE FUNICULAR

Between I. Clark Ádám tér and Castle Hill
bkv.hu/en/buda_castle_funicular

This simple system consists of two carriages that are connected by a rope so that when one is going up, the other is coming down. It links the Buda end of Chain Bridge and Buda Castle. It was opened in 1870 and originally driven by steam. The carriages are called 'Margit' (after the bridge) and 'Gellért' (after the hill).

470 AMPHIBIOUS BUS

V. Széchenyi István tér 7–8
Lipótváros ②
+36 1 332 2555
riverride.com

The privately-owned service called RiverRide covers a route that's half on land, half on water – it was very complicated to get the necessary licences. The vehicle looks like a ship and has had only one accident so far: the engine stopped, but it was safely towed to the bank, and nobody was hurt. It departs from V. Széchenyi tér 7.

469 BUDA CASTLE FUNICULAR

5

SECRETS

even most Budapestians don't know

---

471 THE SECRET OF TROLLEY BUS NO. 70

Trolley buses in Budapest are red and numbered from 70 to 83. The reason is this: the first line that was installed after WWII, made its maiden voyage exactly on the 70th birthday of comrade Stalin – 'a great friend of the Hungarian people', and was given the number 70 in honour of that. In 1990 some people demanded that the numbers of the buses be changed, but somehow that seemed too complicated.

472 THE REASON WHY MARGARET BRIDGE EXPLODED

On 4 November 1944 there was an explosion on Margaret Bridge. It must have been an accident because apart from the passers-by and the people on tramways, about 40 German soldiers died as well – they were installing mines. The explosion was probably caused by a cigarette and a leaking gas pipe. Two months later all the other bridges were destroyed by mines detonated by the German Army.

473 TOLL MONEY ON BRIDGES

Chain Bridge was the first bridge where even noblemen had to pay a toll fee, from 1849 onwards, the year in which it was completed. It was paid for by the banker and the moneylender Yorgos Sinas from Vienna. In 1871 Budapest bought the bridge, but they needed the toll revenue as well, to build three new bridges. The toll was abolished in 1918.

474 WHY THE CITY HALL BUILDING WAS NEVER COMPLETED

This mid-18th-century building originally housed old and ill soldiers. To build the back, a small piece of the city wall would have had to be destroyed, but that permission was never granted, so the building still remains backless. Since 1894 it has been used by the mayor's office. The latest design contest to complete the building was held in 2007, but the construction ideas were later shelved. City Hall is still unfinished.

475 WHY THE ROYAL CASTLE WAS REMODELLED IN THE 1960S

In 1686 the medieval royal castle was ravaged during a siege; afterwards a bigger and bigger palace was built. By 1913 it was as big as it is today, but it was richly adorned with lots of ornaments, many more than today. That's because the communists who restored it insisted on a simpler façade. They also added a 'real dome', which they built of concrete.

5 great
HUGARIAN AUTHORS
worth reading when visiting Budapest

---

476 PÉTER NÁDAS
1942-

This internationally acclaimed prose writer originally trained as a press photographer. He is mostly known for writing voluminous novels – his longest work, *Parallel Stories*, is 1500 pages long. His autobiography concentrates on his childhood and the Jewish roots of his family. He is also a marked critic of present-day Hungary.

477 LÁSZLÓ KRASZNAHORKAI
1954-

Perhaps the most famous Hungarian prose writer these days and winner of the Man Booker International Prize. He tends to use his metaphoric language to depict the lives of underdogs. He was deeply influenced by Japanese culture. His *Baron Wenckheim's Homecoming* (2016) is a black tragicomedy set in his hometown in south-east Hungary.

478 GYÖRGY DRAGOMÁN
1973-

This prolific, much-loved author was 13 when his family moved from Transylvania to a provincial town in western Hungary. His debut novel, *The White King,* is a carefully crafted story about Hungarians living under the hard-line Romanian communism. It was translated in over 30 languages, and then adapted for the screen – the film was produced with a large European budget. He is also a popular lecturer, despite his slight stutter.

479 FERENC MOLNÁR
1878-1952

This comic playwright was born in Budapest and died in New York. His work is still often staged in Hungary. He started his career as a journalist and a prose writer; his classic youth novel *The Paul Street Boys* is still very popular these days in Hungary, but also in Poland and Italy. The Joseph Town locations where some of the novel's scenes are set, are considered mythic shrines by many adults.

480 MAGDA SZABÓ
1917-2007

This prolific writer was popular for many decades; her career went through a short bad patch during the first years of communism, but the later, milder communists loved and pampered her. Many of her books were translated. Her novel *The Door* was turned into a film in 2012, with Helen Mirren as leading actress.

5

WORLD-FAMOUS BUDAPESTIANS

481 ERNŐ RUBIK, INVENTOR
1944-

This design professor invented the Rubik's Cube in 1974; it was meant as a teaching aid but it became phenomenally successful as a toy. Rubik never gave up teaching and became a symbol of great professionalism and of Hungarian inventiveness, whose talent wasn't killed by the frustrating communist system.

482 BÉLA BARTÓK, COMPOSER
1881-1945

This soft-spoken, 20th-century music genius was a pianist and a professor at the Music Academy. He collected a lot of folk music from Hungary and abroad, and he blended folk motifs with his progressive musical ideas. He was a successful opera composer, too. He protested against fascism and emigrated to the US in 1940.

483 FERENC PUSKAS, FOOTBALL PLAYER
1927-2006

The legendary striker of the Hungarian Golden Team of the 1950s. After the 1956 revolution he emigrated to Spain and became the star of Real Madrid. In his old age he returned to Hungary, as an impoverished smiling old man.

484 FRANZ LISZT, COMPOSER
1811-1886

This child prodigy, born into a German-speaking family, grew up to be a star pianist and trend-setting composer. (And the father-in-law of Wagner.) He travelled a lot, but never forgot his roots: he was generous in that he played many concerts for charity, whenever there was a flood or an other problem in his home country. He established the Music Academy in Budapest, and his Budapest apartment is now a lovely small museum.

485 ROBERT CAPA, PHOTOGRAPHER
1913-1954

Budapest-born Endre Friedmann adopted his nickname as his new name – *cápa* means shark in Hungarian, it's a hint at his smile. This charming workaholic became a war photographer and shot some of the most iconic images of the Spanish civil war and later of D-Day. He documented the war damages in Budapest in 1948. He was killed by a mine in Vietnam.

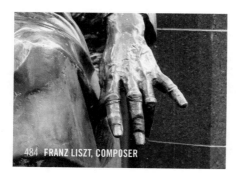

484 FRANZ LISZT, COMPOSER

5 intriguing
MEMORIAL PLAQUES

486 ENDRE TÓT'S MEMORIAL SIGN
VI. Paulay Ede
utca 60.
Terézváros ⑦

'I am happy that once I stood here' – this bronze plaque, sunk into the pavement, is the 'self-memorial' of Endre Tót (1937), an internationally acclaimed Hungarian-born concept artist who lives in Köln. Stand in front of the P60 Gallery to see it. It's a puzzling sentence that gets you thinking.

487 CITY WALL
V. Ferenczy István
utca 26.
Belváros ①

Like any self-respecting medieval town, Pest also had a city wall. A second one was built in the 15th century. It gradually disappeared as blocks of buildings were built against the wall, first on the inside, then on the outside. This elaborate plaque shows where it was: the wall is marked by a metal strip.

488 FLOOD LEVEL MEMORIAL
AT: NATIONAL MUSEUM FENCE
VIII. Bródy
Sándor utca
Józsefváros ⑥

One of the nicest plaques in memory of the flood. The arrow on the tablets shows the actual water height. When the flood came, the National Museum was not here yet – they had barely started to dig the hole for the cellars. It was inaugurated in 1847, the park and the fence were completed in 1879.

489 **1838 FLOOD MAP**
Királyi Pál / Szerb utca
Belváros ①

The terrible flood of 1838 is still deeply imprinted in the collective memory of Budapest. In five days time 151 people died and 2851 houses were destroyed – more than half of all the buildings. This memorial shows the extent of the devastation: the entire area that's white on the plaque was flooded, with the water up to 2,6 metres high in some places.

490 **FIRST KISS: DODÓ AND UBUL**
AT: GLÜCKMANN HOUSE
VII. Rumbach Sebestyén utca 6.
Erzsébetváros ⑦

The text on the plaque reads: 'It was behind this gate that Dodó and Ubul kissed each other on 14 December 1999. Let the house and its inhabitants be blessed! – In honour of the 10th wedding anniversary, by the husband (Ubul) 2011.' This is no joke: many people in Budapest know this smitten husband, a geochemist, and his literary editor wife.

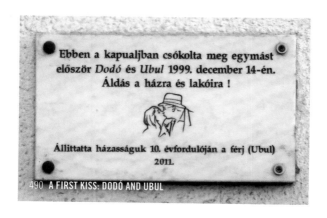

490 A FIRST KISS: DODÓ AND UBUL

5
FILMS
featuring Budapest

---

491 **EVITA**
1996

Most of the outdoor Buenos Aires scenes in this film were shot in downtown Budapest, in the elegant area of Szabadság tér. Just like Buenos Aires, Budapest tried to copy the architecture and city layout of Paris – that's why both cities resemble each other so well. However, in one of the scenes an unmistakeably Hungarian bank sign broke the spell for local moviegoers.

492 **MUNICH**
2005

This epic film commemorated the Israeli sportsmen who were murdered in Munich, by telling the story of the revenge. A group of Mosad agents meticulously hunts down the murderers one by one. The outdoor scenes in Rome, Paris and London, and some in the Netherlands, were all shot in Budapest, in places that will be easily recognised by locals.

493 **BEL AMI**
2012

Everything in downtown Budapest that is so alluring to educated tourists was built in the third part of the 19th century, the period that coincided with the short, comet-like writing career of Guy the Maupassant. The film adaptation of his most famous book was shot in Budapest, near the Opera, in and around a palace in Andrássy.

494 **THE DEBT**
2010

This much-acclaimed British-American film is set in Israel, and tells a story about Israeli Nazi-hunters, one that has been retold many times and turns out to be fundamentally untrue. The final scenes are supposed to be set in Ukraine, but as a matter of fact they were shot in Budapest, namely on Parliament Square and in a large lunatic asylum called Lipótmező.

495 **THE GRAND BUDAPEST HOTEL**
2014

This hilarious, brilliant film by Wes Anderson has a hairbreadth connection with Budapest, the most minimal relation theoretically possible: it has nothing to do with Budapest, except for the title. It is set in a grandiose, glitzy hotel, high in the mountains of Bohemia, then part of the Austro-Hungarian monarchy.

5 examples of
BAD TASTE
in Budapest

---

496 GLADYS VANDERBILT'S VILLA
VI. Andrássy út 104.
Terézváros ⑦⑧

Aristocrat László Széchenyi was so deep in debt that he went to Karlsbad to find a rich heiress. And he succeeded: he married Gladys Vanderbilt in 1908. This villa was given to them as a wedding gift. Now it is the Russian embassy: the Russians built the naff extension on the right.

497 A REAR-VIEW MIRROR ON A MEDIEVAL HOUSE
I. Országház utca 18.
Várnegyed ④

Blocks in the Castle District tend to be district-owned: the Landmark Authority preferred not to privatise them, to be able to protect the architecture from changes. However, a tenant on the first floor of this fine Gothic building felt it appropriate to install a car rear-view mirror outside the window to check the visitors from inside.

498 MADONNA WITH LITTLE JESUS
I. Szent György tér 2.
Várnegyed ④

On the edge of the medieval fortress there is an oversized black statue, erected by a private foundation. It refers to a late-17th-century urban legend. It is so big that it blocks the panorama when seen from behind, and it is too small to be seen from Pest. It has a nickname among the locals: 'Suicidal Madonna'.

499 BUILT-IN BALCONIES, SZŐLŐ UTCA PREFAB BLOCK

III. Szőlő utca
Óbuda ⑩

This monstrous ten-storey prefab block, completed in 1970, is the biggest in the country. It is 338 metres long, that's longer than the Parliament. It comprised no less than 886 (!) apartments. What makes it particularly cheap-looking are the many dozens of balconies that were 'added' to the apartments illegally.

500 ORGANIC EXTENSION OF A BEAUX ARTS BUILDING

VIII. Szentkirályi
utca 18.
Józsefváros ⑥

This two-storey typical building from 1867 was 'upgraded' in 1994 by the organic traditionalist Imre Makovecz (1935-2011): four more storeys were added in a highly tasteless, insensitive manner, and a monster was born. Makovecz was the architect of many iconic buildings; most of them stand by themselves – then the question whether they fit into the architectural context or not is less of an issue.

496 GLADYS VANDERBILT'S VILLA

PARLIAMENT BUILDING

INDEX

DISCARD

COLOPHON

EDITING *and* COMPOSING — András Török

GRAPHIC DESIGN — Joke Gossé and Sarah Schrauwen

PHOTOGRAPHY — András Török — p. 83: Shutterstock

COVER IMAGE — Budapest Zoo (secret 397)

The addresses in this book have been selected after thorough independent research by the author, in collaboration with Luster Publishers. The selection is solely based on personal evaluation of the business by the author. Nothing in this book was published in exchange for payment or benefits of any kind.

D/2018/12.005/1
ISBN 978 94 6058 2172
NUR 510, 512

© 2018 Luster, Antwerp
www.lusterweb.com — www.the500hiddensecrets.com
info@lusterweb.com

Printed in Italy by Printer Trento.